THE STOR
KEEPER OF THE 'C

Part of The Mind Coach® Series

Marilyne Woodsmall, Ph.M.

A SELECTION OF OTHER WORKS

The Mind Coach® Series CDs: Part I
The Story of Jaren: Keeper of the Clean Heart Grid'®
www.mindbraintechnologies.com

The Mind Coach® Series Star Performance Manual:
Unlocking the Power of Your Truth
www.mindbraintechnologies.com

The Future of Learning: The Michel Thomas Method
Freeing Minds One Person at a Time
www.themichelthomasmethod.com
www.thefutureoflearning.com

People Pattern™ Power: The Nine Keys to Business Success
www.peoplepatternpower.com

The People Pattern™ Prayers:
What You've Always Wanted, But Were Afraid To Ask For
www.thescienceofidiots.com

On the Wings of Angels: Inspirational Truths

Red Alert: The Culture Crisis -
Implications of the General Developmental Model

Learning How to Learn™:
Cultivating our Children for the Future

Motive: The Secret Key to Influence

The Secrets to Motivation in the Workplace

Behavioral Assessment Tools:
Profiling Plus™ - Hiring Right
The Value Culture™ Profile
The People Pattern™ Profile
The Entrecode™ Profile

THE STORY OF JAREN: KEEPER OF THE 'CLEAN HEART GRID'®

Part of The Mind Coach® Series

Marilyne Woodsmall, Ph.M.
Next Step Press

THE STORY OF JAREN:
KEEPER OF THE 'CLEAN HEART GRID'®

DEDICATION

I dedicate this to my precious felines, Snowy, Sammy, Ninja, and Minow, to Master Poufy in spirit, to Mr. Kitty, and to our animal companions everywhere, as well as to the star children coming into the world, all of whom embody the essence of unconditional love and are of "*clean heart*."

CONTENTS

FORWARD

The world in which we live is constantly changing, and at a faster pace than ever before. Technological advances constantly bombard us with endless information, much of which distracts us from what really matters in life. And yet, amid the flux, there is a constant. It is that people in all walks of life and all ages, still strive to achieve success in one form or another in their personal or professional lives.

Parents would like to see their children excel and to stand out from the crowd. Business people everywhere go all out to be profitable and successful in their respective fields. Athletes endeavor to be at the top of their sport. Celebrities crave the spotlight and want their work to outshine that of others.

However, there is a major change occurring, subtle to some and yet quite obvious to others. It is that success has taken on a new meaning. Old patterns of behavior and past paradigms in all areas of our lives are either no longer relevant or are no longer effective. One of the most far-reaching of these paradigms has to do with how we define and reward success. Some of us have known this new paradigm all along and some are just discovering it.

In the past, the particular skills that would enable a person to succeed both in the business world and in life are no longer the gauge by which to teach our children, nor are they the way to get ahead. In fact, research demonstrates that so called emotional intelligence and social intelligence are more important than IQ when it comes to true success in life.

There is something far more significant and more powerful that will change the way we evaluate true "success" in the workplace and in society at large. Success will be measured by one's ability to experience life from the heart, and as such, the

FORWARD

oneness of all things in the Universe. I call this new paradigm for success to be of "*clean heart*."

And this is the core of "*The Story of Jaren: Keeper of the 'Clean Heart Grid'®*".

When I first wrote this story in the 1990's, there were those who were not ready for the message. It is because so many were still operating from the mind and not from the heart. Times are very different now. In the words of the *Mind Coach*®: "There are no coincidences in this world. There is only Divine Timing, pure and simple." And the time has come for this heart-based awareness and for being of "*clean heart*" to lead the way as the new paradigm for success in the new energetic landscape.

Are you ready, now, to find out how?

Marilyne Woodsmall, Ph.M.
The Mind Coach®

THE STORY OF JAREN:
KEEPER OF THE 'CLEAN HEART GRID'®

INTRODUCTION:

UNLOCKING THE POWER OF YOUR TRUTH

The Story of Jaren: Keeper of the 'Clean Heart Grid®" is part of my *Mind Coach® Series* and is an educational/inspirational story and journey of self-discovery and personal growth.

It all began in 1990 when I would write stories as a trainer to make it easier for students to assimilate the teachings. Then soon afterwards, when I began working with Olympic Athletes and Olympic Coaches, first modeling "the elite among the elite" and then training and coaching them for competition, I decided to enhance my storytelling by using a powerful teaching model called *"layering."*

THE STORY OF JAREN:
KEEPER OF THE 'CLEAN HEART GRID'®

In this story, I present the golden nuggets or secrets of this "elite performance" using this model of "layered learning." Think of it as multi-tasked learning that occurs without consciously doing anything to learn. You don't even have to take notes to learn what I am teaching you in this story. You simply experience each "parcel of wisdom" and each Defining Moment and move onto the next one. Many parents have told me how they have used *The Story of Jaren* to teach their children certain concepts easily, have them understand them, and make it fun at the same time. This happened to be one of my goals in writing this story so many years ago.

The question arises...why teach in story form? There are several reasons for sharing my several decades of modeling knowledge and behavioral change technology in a story form.

1) First, there is always so much knowledge to transfer in trainings, particularly in our model-based trainings; and **a story is the ideal form in which to integrate the teachings and make the learnings easily accessible**.

2) Second, in my work and research in learning, I know that **learning occurs best when there is no tension in the**

INTRODUCTION

mind/body. So a story would be an ideal way to make learning fun and effortless without worrying about "trying to remember" the information through worthless memorization. First and foremost, learning should be fun. (www.thefutureoflearning.com)

3) Third, it is easier for the unconscious mind to take in information than the conscious mind. And **a story ideally lends itself to reaching the unconscious mind**. This form is all the more powerful because the subconscious mind acts like a sponge, retaining every single thought, word, picture, feeling, sound, etc., that passes into it whether we are consciously aware of it or not. As the *Mind Coach®* in this story, I teach you step by step how to monitor your mind and body. You learn how to become aware of thoughts, feelings, pictures, words, sounds, etc., that may impact your performance and ultimately change the nature of what may be your defining moment.

4) Fourth, there is a secret I'd like to share with you which is another reason why I decided to transfer this information

in a story. The secret is this: **the most effective way in which to communicate with the unconscious mind is through pictures**. And a story is such an efficient way to reach the unconscious mind because in reading or in listening to a story one has to create pictures in the mind in order to make sense of the words (I also recorded *The Story of Jaren: Keeper of the 'Clean Heart Grid'®"* as a CD set in the 1990's. (www.mindbraintechnologies.com).

5) Fifth, in our present day world, attention spans are dwindling every minute. I realized that **a story would be a good way to help readers/listeners to maintain focus** and at the same time be certain that the knowledge be assimilated with ease.

6) Last and certainly not least, I wanted to create a powerful story that synthesizes:

a) **the proven know-how of superior performance experts** which I extracted through our behavioral modeling process,

INTRODUCTION

b) what I call ***"ancient wisdom of the ages,"*** and

c) real-life practical information and insights about "character-building" in a world that has lost touch with what really matters in life.

The result is a story that teaches you powerful tools for behavioral change to help you, your children, your family, your colleagues, and your friends, to "think" in a new way. It provides an effective blueprint in our increasingly competitive world for achieving true success based on the *"Clean Heart Grid"*® paradigm. Furthermore, it is a story that teaches you how to access your inner reserves of power to be the best that you can be on your chosen path in life.

With *"The Story of Jaren: Keeper of the Clean Heart Grid'®"*, you now have a practical template of information and wisdom that I have been using with *elite performers* for years to bring them to even higher levels of performance enhancement. Furthermore, as you will see, I give you practical and effective tools to guide you to a mastery of your mind, your emotions, your body, your spirit, and thus, your being. To accomplish this, I have created a learning template that incorporates both the *"what"* and the *"how to."* Knowing what to do is only part of the picture. You must also know how to do something in order to succeed. And it is the latter that is missing from most of the self-help material out there.

As the *Mind Coach®*, I teach you what I call *"The Laws of Elite Performance"*™ (aka, *"The Nine Mind Energies"*™) which I based on my work in professionally modeling, training and coaching top performers in many fields, including Olympic athletes and Olympic coaches, top entrepreneurs, top educators (including the man whom I consider to have been the greatest educator of the past fifty plus years), top salespeople, and more.

I have found that no matter what the task or performance context involved, there are basic characteristics shared by superior performers which make the difference between mediocre performance and *Elite Performance*. What I found was that these qualities come from deep within you, from what I call your place of Truth. It is these very qualities of perfect performance – coming from your place of Truth, which I am now sharing with you. In so

INTRODUCTION

doing, you are learning how to "Unlock the Power of Your Truth" and you are honoring your true essence as well.

As you work through *The Story of Jaren*, you will discover the qualities or Truths that lie deep within yourself. **These are Your Truths.** Most of the time, these Truths are outside of your conscious awareness, just as they often are with the *elite performers* and clients with whom I work. You are no different from these *elite performers*. You also have Your Truths lying inside of you. In *The Story of Jaren*, I will teach you how to bring them into your conscious awareness, just as I have taught so many others to do so over the years.

Why does this method work? It works because these Truths, presented as *"The Nine Mind Energies"*™, are not based on someone's theory of what works, or on what experts think that they are doing. *"The Laws of Elite Performance"*™ are based my professionally modeling what experts and superior performers actually do (their *"unconscious competency"*) in accomplishing their tasks in often flawless fashion. It is these reality-based qualities of top performers, which I am now sharing with you. I lead you to the discovery of these *Laws* or *"Mind Energies™*, as I named them, that have been living inside of you all along, outside of your conscious "knowing."

You may be asking yourself "why" the word *energies*? It has to do with what is known as The Law of Vibration. In the words of *The Mind Coach®*: "Everything in the Universe is vibration, everything." I have been teaching The Law of Vibration and other metaphysical wisdom for twenty plus years. Early on in the 1990's, in teaching this, there were those who simply did not "get it," for they were not ready for this kind of information.

Now times have changed. There is a marked shift in values that corresponds to the shift of consciousness that is occurring. This shift is connected to the new success paradigm I discussed earlier in the Forward. This shift along with some trendy psycho-spiritual writings in vogue, have made this information about the nature of our thoughts as vibration more mainstream than ever before.

Unlike the some of the all the rage new-age writings, the lessons of *"The Story of Jaren"* are not about manifesting

INTRODUCTION

narcissistic or greed-based desires using The Law of Attraction. The lessons here, again all in story form, are of a noble nature in that you will understand what really matters when it comes to success. Here you will also learn about how our very thoughts, our internal imagery and our inner feelings are all vibrationally based and correspond to *The Law of Vibration*. Among other things, you will also learn how to identify, to control and to change these various elements of the mind and body to work as your personal ally rather than as your enemy.

Interestingly, this concept of vibration is nothing new to quantum physicists. For years they have been aware of the fact that everything in the universe is vibration. It is just in recent years, however, that this knowledge is being disseminated to the public at large.

As you learn these secrets to superior performance in this story, you, your children, your friends, your colleagues, etc. can know what it takes to excel and to enhance your personal growth as well. And yet this is merely a beginning. For "elite performance" is just the first step towards true success. You will also discover what I call *"The Divine Nine Laws of Star Performance"™*. *The Divine Nine™*, as I also refer to them, represent the higher principles connected to the *"Clean Heart Grid"®* that go far beyond personal performance in the grand scheme of things called life.

"The Divine Nine Laws"™ guide you to the next level of performance --- to the level of Truth that goes beyond your personal place of Truth. They take you to a higher level of awareness...to the level of Universal Truth and Universal Laws. This is a path that is more mystical, more metaphysical in nature so it is definitely not for everyone. There are those who "get it," just as there are those who "don't get it" and those who never will.

Timing is everything in life. There comes a time when we are more receptive to certain ideas and willing to grow to new levels. That is why you now have this information within your grasp.

"The Divine Nine Laws of Star Performance"™ will change the way you see the world around you. They will nurture the seeds of your mission that have been inside your place of Truth all these years. They will bring you to a new level of being: that of *Star*

INTRODUCTION

Performer, one who is here to make a difference in this world. Are you ready?

Now, let Jaren and the *Mind Coach®* teach you the secrets of top performers and lead you to a *new way of thinking about yourself, about our world* and *about your place in it.* As you unlock the power of your truth, you too, will learn to be of "***clean heart***"; and you will discover what it takes to be a true *Star Performer* in your own right. In so doing, we will all do our part in making this a better world...a world in which we achieve the awareness that *all is one, and one is all* in the new energetic landscape.

With gracious gratitude,

The Mind Coach®

CHAPTER I

THE SECRET OF THE *'CLEAN HEART GRID'*®

Dear Ones, do you remember when...and probably not...

A long time ago, at a time when time was not even of the essence, where...in an enchanted land, a place far, far away, and at the same time very close to our hearts...some remarkable events took place?

Do you remember this land?

It was truly a wondrous place of endless possibilities and opportunities, an extraordinary land where a select group of people always strove to excel in the performance of a particular talent.

In fact, every several years this select group would come

together to hold a series of *Great Games* to test their special skills. This was a time of immense joy for some and terrible disappointment for others. This could have been a time of sheer delight and jubilation for all, if only they had been blessed with the desire to seek wisdom and to become greater in ways not measured by material success.

There was one in this land who was especially blessed, a young, aspiring performer named JAREN. And his name was no accident, for there are no coincidences in this world. And it is no coincidence that this story is now being told. For the time has come for uplifting transformation to occur on our planet...the time has come to shine the light of wisdom all across the land...the time has come to ring the bell of peace and harmony throughout...the time has come to guide many new souls onto the path of spiritual enlightenment. Yes, the time has come...for now marks the date of the *Great Games* once again!

At last, it is time to tell this story to help many on the path who, like aspiring Jaren, would like to be blessed with the wisdom of a special mentor; one who will help them find the keys to unlock their personal treasure chest and become the Eternal Celestial Jewels they are meant to be --- with a mentor who will transform their most cherished dreams into a tangible reality, by activating powers within which were previously inaccessible at will.

Now, in this land, there happened to be a rather unusual Wise Person, an enchanting Lady known for her magical ways called the *Mind Coach*®. One day, in his quest for keys to unlock the mysteries of perfect performance, Jaren discovered her, not by accident, of course, for there are no coincidences in this world. Word had long ago spread throughout the land that this wise Wizardress concocted a series of Magical Formulas which enable people to achieve perfect performance and to be their best by evolving in very special ways.

Jaren knew that he had to meet this Wise Lady, no matter what. She had a certain magic mental touch which others failed to imitate, no matter how hard they tried. So Jaren knew it was important to go directly to the source of this mental magic --- to this Wise Lady, to the *Mind Coach*® herself, to the creator of the Magic Formulas. Jaren knew, somehow, in his heart that he was destined

THE STORY OF JAREN:
KEEPER OF THE 'CLEAN HEART GRID'®

to partake of her wisdom, although the real connection between him and the *Mind Coach*® was to be revealed at a later time, as we shall see. Jaren also knew that every moment was precious, since the time of the *Great Games* was quickly approaching.

So Jaren set off on a new quest that would change his life forever in a manner he had never dreamed possible.....while the mighty force of Divine Will lit the spark that was to shine the light of a brilliant destiny all across the sky!

Dear Ones, now take a gentle, deep breath, relax and take a wonderful trip through time to the land of the *Mind Coach*®; and witness her pillars of wisdom marking the sacred site where blessings from Above abound. Be Jaren's companion on his journey of magical discovery, that is, after all, an enchanting discovery of the power within all of us, isn't it!?! Accompany Jaren on his visit to the Wise Lady.

Won't you take in, Dear Ones, the gentle words of the *Mind Coach*® as she guides you as well, to your place in the sky, to a place where your dreams become a reality, NOW that you feel, touch, see and understand to be yours forever..!

THE SECRET OF THE *'CLEAN HEART GRID'*®

Jaren set forth on his travels totally ecstatic about his upcoming encounter with the *Mind Coach*®. He traveled miles and miles on his quest, curiously accompanied by the sweet, soothing sounds of a gently strummed harp.

"Am I going mad?" exclaimed Jaren.

As Jaren pondered aloud, he realized that the Angelic Celestial Beauties from high above among the clouds were musically guiding him to his destination. The closer he got to the realm of the *Mind Coach*®, the louder the notes reverberated in his head. After a long journey, he joyfully arrived at the wonderful place where the Wise Lady worked her Magic. As Jaren approached, he looked up to see a glorious rainbow glistening above him, like the multi-colored halos worn by the winged Celestial Companions from Above.

Suddenly, out of nowhere, a gentle breeze permeated the air with the fragrant scent of carnations and camellias. There she appeared before him, her almond eyes twinkling with delight, her head and shoulders held high in a regal and dignified stance, welcoming him with her hands cupped to her *Heart Center*, and bowing her head. Jaren was overjoyed, finally, to be in the company of the fabled *Mind Coach®*. After taking a minute to collect himself he approached her and immediately felt a warm, throbbing sensation in his heart center.

"It's really curious," he wondered silently to himself. "From the moment I heard about the *Mind Coach®*, I have been feeling that sensation of pulsating warmth in my chest, and now it's so intense that..."

His silent thoughts were quickly overtaken by her poised, commanding presence and by the look of erudition, in her penetrating eyes. Her gentle smile and unassuming air immediately put him at ease.

In a way, he was surprised to find the *Mind Coach®* to be so accessible; and at the same time, he had somehow known all along that she would be cordial, confident and calm. He was elated to look finally upon the elegant Wise Lady. She was dressed in a long, ivory-white flowing gown that shimmered with little gold stars embroidered onto it. Her matching star-shaped earrings accentuated the tiny glittery stars perfectly placed in her upswept hair; and from a beautiful gold choker around her neck dangled an intriguing symbol in gold.

At this point in time, there was no way that Jaren dared ask her the meaning of the exquisite pendant, even though his curiosity was piqued more than ever. He felt so relaxed to be in her company. There was a certain graceful radiance about her that he had never experienced before. He was not accustomed to being in the presence of a true Lady! And he was so grateful for the sudden sense of calm he felt throughout his body, a serenity created by her soothing presence and kind manner. At that moment, Jaren realized that he had never experienced such a feeling of inner peace; and he kept this thought to himself.

"Can you help me, dear *Mind Coach*®?" asked Jaren, in a rather subdued tone of voice.

With a humbled expression on his face, Jaren appeared to be completely captivated by her dignified demeanor which seemed to reinforce the mysterious aura surrounding her. The wise *Mind Coach*® responded with a fixed, discerning gaze that seemed to see right through him and did. She then began to speak with her hands cupped at her *Heart Center*.

"In more ways than you could ever imagine at this time....

YOU are the Dear One, young person! It is no accident that you have come to see me, for there are no coincidences in this world. There is only Divine Timing, pure and simple! Our lovely, Celestial Angelic Companions from Above, confirmed that with their beautiful rainbow halo painted in the sky marking this place! They are Divine Messengers to signal that I am here to reveal to you the special Mission of your soul."

With this iteration, the *Mind Coach*® looked up to the Heavens, as if to connect with Spirit, the vibration of Infinite Intelligence, beaming Light and Wisdom back to Jaren.

"You see, Dear One, every soul has its particular Mission. Some are aware of their Mission, while others are not, and perhaps may never be in this lifetime. With my guidance, you are to discover your own personal Mission; and I am here to help you become the vessel that I now am. You see, my wisdom and powers are not really mine, Dear One. They are simply the miraculous gifts of Spirit flowing through me, and I may share my gifts with others who are ready to receive them. The mere fact that you have searched me out is the first sign that you are already on the enlightened path. Only those who truly possess a strong desire to evolve and who are good, positive souls who are willing to help others can enter my Sacred Circle....

....There are many people in this land sadly living their lives in a dark cloud of rage, or who are carried off by the mighty wind of narcissism, and still others who are enveloped by the Scylla and Charybdis swift, swirling whirlpool of greed. They, too, are not ready to join my Sacred Circle."

Jaren reflected for a time and then with a knowing look in his eyes, announced:

"I know that I am meant to be here with you, wise *Mind Coach*®, to learn how to help open the eyes of the people of whom you now speak. I want so much to show them just how their unenlightened behaviors block their path to spiritual growth! On a certain level, I guess I've known for awhile that my path to success was connected in some manner to my spiritual awakening; and I am beginning, thankfully, to see the Light."

THE STORY OF JAREN:
KEEPER OF THE 'CLEAN HEART GRID'®

The *Mind Coach*® expected this very response, for she had in her own heart, foreseen his coming to her. In fact, she had read his heart upon the very moment her eyes were cast upon his being. The Wise Lady proceeded with her discourse.

"Dear One, your words are much more prophetic than you realize right now, for I guarantee that you will see a Light --- a very special Light --- indeed, when the time is right, not a second before, not a second after. Know that our land was not like this in eras past. In recent times, however, terrible forces fueled by greed and ego increasingly bombard people all over the land with a steady barrage of furiously brutal, viciously violent and crudely offensive images and sounds. Dear One, you have seen just how the natural light of many around you is tainted and dimmed by these far from positive influences which intoxicate their ♥ minds ♥ bodies ♥ souls ♥ and ♥ spirits ♥ like corruptive toxins that in fact, poison the very lifeblood running through their bodies. And, if among them, there are aspiring ones seeking what they blindly deem as success, they will remain spiritual vacuums until they change to let in the LIGHT once again."

THE SECRET OF THE *'CLEAN HEART GRID'*®

Her words seemed to kindle a burst of sunshine, in Jaren's face, as he exclaimed politely:

"Wise Lady, I have heard that you have a way of dealing with such negativity. I have heard that you, the good Wizardress that you are, distinguish yourself as a Master of the Laws of Energy."

The *Mind Coach*® smiled with a sweet twinkle in her eyes as she continued to speak.

"You have heard by now, Dear One, that I am a very discreet person who is quite selective about the type of individuals whom I let into my Sacred Circle. I may help many from afar and as an Energetic Master, I necessarily make certain that who and what surround me in my Inner Circle are always positive and untainted. In fact, I have turned many away who were not sincere and honest in their essence. What you must remember is that every soul has a vibration associated with it, a *vibrational calling card*™, so to speak, that is different for each and every soul. I refer to positive energy as *posivations*™. If I sense negative energy or negative vibrations which I call *negavations*™ in any way, then that person has no chance of sharing the wisdom of my Inner Circle at the present time. I always send these souls a ball of Light from Spirit which will spark at least a tiny ray of kindness within them, even if only for a moment. The *posivations*™ do leave their mark and the love emanating from them does eventually conquer all, even if it takes awhile. And, yes, I can detect and identify all vibrations both near and from afar. As for the negative forces, I will teach you when the time is right, just how to perceive them, then how to neutralize their negative effect on whatever is within their energetic reach, and beyond."

"I am so relieved to hear what you have said about these vibrations because I've thought myself to be a bit crazy at times when I sense certain things about people that others do not. Thank you for opening my heart to your wisdom by allowing me to be part of your Sacred Circle, precious *Mind Coach*®," exclaimed young Jaren with joyous gratitude in his voice.

"Once again, your words are more prophetic than you could ever know right now. It is I who THANK YOU, Dear One, for you are a precious gift to me. It is I who am honored by your presence! Know, too, Dear One, that you are blessed with great gifts from the

THE SECRET OF THE *'CLEAN HEART GRID'*®

Universe --- with talent, with clarity of purpose and with virtue as well. Believe me....that is a rare combination in our land where ego, falsity and greed often reign supreme among many, particularly among those perceived to be most successful. Beware of anger, bitterness, fear, and ego for they will muddy the heart by blocking rays of goodness from entering it."

"Kind and wise *Mind Coach*®, your soothing voice seems to blend with the melodious sounds of the harp chords we are hearing from Above," declared Jaren.

"That is no accident for there are no coincidences in this world. These lovely tones are meant to be a constant reminder of the very special connection that you and I share together. Dear One, know that you and I share a beautiful secret, a unique and precious blessing, and one which is perhaps the greatest gift offered by Spirit: the gift of a *'CLEAN HEART.'* *Ena Binati*. Take heed, Dear One. *Ena Binati*."

Upon uttering these strange words, the *Mind Coach*® placed her cupped hands to her Heart Center and resumed her declaration.

THE STORY OF JAREN:
KEEPER OF THE 'CLEAN HEART GRID'®

"Dear One, you are blessed with a 'clean heart' in every aspect of your being: in your ♥ body ♥ in your ♥ mind ♥ in your ♥ soul ♥ and in your ♥ spirit ♥. Entwined around this Heart of Love are three golden cords of phenomenal power."

Jaren listened with intensity marveling at each word uttered by the graceful Wizardress, beaming with modest excitement as she continued to speak with a penetrating gaze of love and compassion. Suddenly, he felt a tingling energy spiraling within him when the *Mind Coach®* gestured her hands in three distinct movements, three times around his body. He even thought he saw a subtle light twinkling as it traced the movement of her hands.

"These cords embody the three qualities required to ennoble a human soul on this earth." declared the *Mind Coach®* with joy. "Together, these three qualities constitute a powerful force known as *The Tri-Essence Vibration™* which is the *energynetic core™* of a 'clean heart'. This magnificent *Tri-essence Vibration™* is comprised of RESPECT, INTEGRITY and DIGNITY which blend together in one, smooth *synergynetic flow™*. You will understand the significance of this vibrational flow by the end of this day. For now, know, Dear One, that it is this *Tri-essence Vibration*™ which elevates a *'clean heart'* above all of the unenlightened souls --- above those in our land who are living out a culture of rage in one form or another."

"I am both grateful and humbled by what you are saying," declared Jaren. "How is it that I am blessed with such a noble gift? I am in such awe that I have no words to express what I am feeling right now."

"Your choice of words confirms, many times over that you are of *'clean heart.'* You are free of arrogance, anger and deceit. You exemplify nobility of thought, feeling and action which shines through in your *Tri-essence Vibration*™ in the following ways. First, you respect every cell of your being and others. You are considerate and kind towards all living creatures. You especially cherish all of our dear animal companions who share our land. You respect all things animate and inanimate. You are committed to help all those in need, whether emotional, physical or spiritual need; and you are first to come to the assistance of those in danger, no matter what the source of the danger, regardless of any personal peril to you. You are proud of your land and your wear that pride in all that you do. Moreover, you respect and protect Mother Earth in all of her manifestations. You show great care for our environment and your actions reflect this concern.

Second, you are honest. You demonstrate great strength of character, as shown by your strong sense of integrity. Sound ethical fibers run throughout your mind, body, soul and spirit. You are trustworthy and sincere every moment of every day.

And, third, of course, you choose to act with great dignity of self in all that you do, whether alone or in the company of others. In short, you are of 'clean heart' in every aspect of your being."

"Now I see why some of my peers have fallen short of the mark, so to speak," chimed in Jaren. "And, wise *Mind Coach®,* I am proud to be who I am, even if there are some who might think that disrespectful, selfish or unkind acts, are a sign of power."

The elegant Lady gracefully acknowledged the sincerity in Jaren's voice and the clarity of his words by raising her cupped hands to her *Heart Center,* and bowing her head as she had done when her eyes met his eager gaze and she read his 'clean heart' for the first time.

"Dear One," she continued, "as I have already told you, true power does not lie in vile places. Without the qualities of RESPECT, INTEGRITY and DIGNITY, true power cannot be made manifest. We live in a time in which the pace of everything is quickening at an exponential rate, in more ways, and on more levels than you can even fathom right now. The rapidly expanding invasion of mindless diversions in this land has grown into a major malignancy which is profoundly and unconsciously lowering the vibrations of the masses who partake of it. That is why *The Tri-essence Vibration*™ is so deficient at this time."

"I want so much to help these people, to open their eyes to what really matters in life. I, too, will send them balls of Light!" Jaren proclaimed, with a tinge of hopeful exuberance in his voice.

"Lovely...Lovely...Lovely," whispered the wise *Mind Coach*®. "Because you are of 'clean heart' you do not judge. Because you are of 'clean heart', you show compassion and a genuine desire to help others to see the LIGHT. As such, you set a golden example for those perceptive enough to understand and to follow. Be not shaken by those who turn away, Dear One, or by those who ridicule that which they cannot understand at this time for they are not yet ready for the message."

"Expressing kindness and goodness is the only way I choose to act and I am proud to be that way," cheered Jaren. I truly am thankful for being who I am, even if I still have far to go on my path," he added rather modestly.

"Dear One, we are all constantly evolving in the way in which we are meant to do so at any given stage in our lives. Such work is never done. Know, Dear One, *'clean heart'* that you are, that with my guidance I will teach you to become a brilliant star with a special Light that shines in extraordinary ways."

Jaren listened attentively with a look in his eyes that confirmed all that the *Mind Coach*® was saying, and then added:

"Dear *Mind Coach*®, I've worked long and hard practicing many hours on a demanding schedule. And yet, I've always felt that something was missing. On some days I do really well and on other days I do poorly. I don't know why."

"I will teach you the secrets that differentiate between

excellence and mediocrity. With my help you will become a lasting star in your own right, far beyond the passing of the *Great Games*. I will teach you the magic keys that will enable you to transition quickly and easily, between occasional good performances and consistent brilliant performances."

"Do these keys have anything to do with the Magical Formulas of which I have heard so much? Please tell me more, dear *Mind Coach*®," Jaren asked politely.

"Indeed. I see you have been told only part of the story," she said. "There is more although you will not hear it all completely at this time. You have heard that for many years I have developed and pursued the strange and unusual task of figuring out how great performers do what they do. I have always asked myself, 'How is it possible that some excel while others do not?' I found many answers and I continued to develop and expand the method. The result has been my creation of a series of unique formulas which I customize to fit the different people with whom I work. I organize these formulas in such a way as to pass them on to selected others in various fields. For many years now, I have combined my cutting edge *'Mind-Magic Technology'*™ with what I refer to as insightful 'wisdom of the ages'."

"Oh, *Mind Coach*®, I want so much for you to teach me personally how to use the formulas that are right for me. The *Great Games* will soon be upon us. And I want to really shine!" exclaimed Jaren. "When I compete I often win, yet I don't always seem to get into my perfect rhythm in which to perform my skill as I would like. If only I could just do as well in competition as in my best practices! It's not just about winning because even when I do win, I always feel that there is another power at work inside of me."

"Precisely, Dear One! It is that very power which we will nourish and direct together. Most of those around you are totally unaware of this power. Mere winning is not the true measure of success! You will soon know why when you make your mark high above in the sky. That I promise you, Dear One. And I do keep my promises," affirmed the *Mind Coach*® in an authoritative voice.

"Please teach me the magic formulas which are right for me," Jaren asked again with great respect for the *Mind Coach*®.

"Only because your ego is free of the venomous daggers of

vanity, can I teach you part of the formulas. The 'ancient wisdom of the ages' is not for the ego driven in this world," she continued to say. "It is not for the irreverent of Spirit. It is not for the dishonest. It is not for the undignified. In short, it is only for those who are of 'clean heart.' Remember that Spirit works in wondrous ways and will not provide this knowledge to those who are not ready to hear it. That is why there are some, as you know, who refuse to listen to this wisdom. They are not meant to hear it because they cannot understand it at this time."

Jaren's polite ways truly distinguished him from many other young people in this land, and the *Mind Coach*® acknowledged this by gracefully moving her cupped hands to her *Heart Center* once again, bowing her head, as she made a sacred gesture.

Strangely, yet not so strangely, after all, the soothing sounds of harp chords began to filter through the air sounding louder than before, as the *Mind Coach*® uttered more of her wisdom. At the very same moment, the rays of the sun seemed to shine even more brightly; and the gorgeous, glistening, multi-colored halos emerged once again from behind a radiant, billowy cloud.

THE STORY OF JAREN:
KEEPER OF THE 'CLEAN HEART GRID'®

"Dear One, 'clean heart' that you are, as you can see and hear, Divine Timing in all of its splendor has marked your arrival here to me in a rather distinctive manner! It is no accident that I have spent a good deal of time discussing the significance of a 'clean heart' and explaining why it is a rarity in this land. There is more to our 'clean heart' exchange than meets the physical eye. The time has come, Dear One, for me to reveal the real reason why you have so desired to seek me out, for I am to reveal to you a secret that you have held for many ages, deep within every cell of your being --- deep within your physical, mental, emotional and spiritual bodies --- a secret *energynetic code*™ that has been emblazoned on your soul since its creation."

Her gentle words continued to mesh in perfect rhythm with the harmonious harp chords that caressed the air around them.

"The secret is this:

THE SECRET OF THE *'CLEAN HEART GRID'*®

Like every powerful force in the Universe, *The Tri-essence Vibration*™ is guarded by special, gifted individuals who are predestined to be its protectors and guardians. This *Tri-essence Vibration*™ resides in a sacred place called *'THE CLEAN HEART GRID'*®. And Jaren, *'clean heart'* that you are, YOU and only YOU, are meant to take my place as the next guardian of this incredibly powerful Grid! You, *Jaren*, are next in line to uphold this *sacred vibration* as *Keeper of 'The Clean Heart Grid'*®. This will not occur for some time and as the present *Keeper of 'The Clean Heart Grid'*®, I have the privilege today of honoring your soul through Spirit, in a special way as you acknowledge your acceptance of this venerated blessing. *Onunti azanti*, Dear One."

Jaren gave the *Mind Coach*® a rather inquisitive look upon hearing these strange words, and after acknowledging his baffled expression with a quick wink of her eye, she proceeded on. Her look communicated that the time would come to learn the meaning of this utterance.

"From this day forth," she proudly proclaimed, "I will guide you in the fulfillment of this precious mission; and in the name of the

THE STORY OF JAREN:
KEEPER OF THE 'CLEAN HEART GRID'®

Great Light of Spirit in the Universe, I am honored to bestow this blessing upon you. Dear One, this marks the period of your apprenticeship during which time I am to teach you all that I know about *The Tri-essence Vibration*™ and *'The Clean Heart Grid'*®, so that you may one day take charge as its guardian until the passing of the blessing to the soul whose destiny it is to receive it after you. Once you have completed your apprenticeship, we will together take part in a powerful ceremony called the *Corapurvi*. Until then, may Spirit guide you always to use this extraordinary *'Clean Heart Grid'*® as a Divine Beacon to illuminate the way for others to a higher level of being."

Jaren listened closely with glistening tears falling from his awestruck eyes, deeply touched, by the poignant words thus spoken. He sat there speechless. The *Mind Coach*® gave him a reassuring smile and it was obvious that she, too, was visibly moved and so delighted to be the mentor of such a beautiful young soul. With her usual graceful movements, the *Mind Coach*® stood up, her elegant ivory-white gown blowing in the soft breeze. She tightly grasped that exquisite pendant she was wearing around her neck with her right hand. She next placed her left hand upon her *Heart Center*, whispered a prayer under her breath, and made a series of mysterious, circular gestures without alluding at all to their significance.

"Dear One, I will some day soon be able to pass on this prayer to you as well as the many powerful *mudra* and rituals I perform, and not until you have learned much more. Know, Dear One, that this remarkable Grid has been playing a major role in your entire life in all that you have accomplished and in all that you have not accomplished thus far, for that matter. Even the choice of your name, Jaren, is important in its own way, for in your name you carry the vibration of your great ancestor, Jenar, the wise and magnanimous leader of our land eons ago, a leader, who, in his time, served as *Keeper* of *'The Clean Heart Grid'*®. *The Tri-essence Vibration*™ is contained in the *energynetic code*™ of your lineage, that of the powerful and distinguished *House of Jenari*. It is this code which set you in my direction in the first place, acting like a powerful spiritual compass. Your goal to win in the *Great Games* is simply the conscious means to another end, an end that has been residing in your unconscious mind from the moment your soul entered into this life. This end is that of your apprenticeship as the future *Keeper of 'The Clean Heart Grid'®*."

Jaren was still choked up and he found it difficult to get the words out of his mouth.

"Wise *Mind Coach*®, is that why I feel that sensation of intense warmth in my heart? Forgive me for asking a stupid question, as I really do know the answer. And here I thought that I was coming to see you in order to learn how to perform well consistently so that I could win in the *Great Games*. Is it silly of me to ask where to find '*The Clean Heart Grid'®*?"

"*First*, know that in all of our interactions there is no such thing as a silly question. Stupidity arises from not seeking the much needed answers. Ignorance is not bliss, contrary to popular belief," she affirmed in a louder tonality. "Second, know that it is your '*energynetic vibration*'™, that of the powerful and distinguished *House of Jenari*, which is the source of the warm quivers in your heart center which you have been experiencing ever since you heard my name. Third, know, Dear One, that when the time is right, the location of *'The Clean Heart Grid'*® will be revealed to you and you alone. And at an even later time, I will unravel before your unbelieving eyes and ears the entire *Legend of 'The Clean Heart Grid'*®, a stirringly beautiful tale indeed. That must wait."

Upon uttering these words, the *Mind Coach*® stood up and cupped her hands at her *Heart Center* once again, and declared in a rather authoritative tone of voice:

"Ena Binati. Take heed, Dear One. *Ena Binati.* 'Clean heart' that you are, you now consciously carry these utterances with you wherever you go, as you travel throughout eternity:

True Success in life is not measured

by material gain...

True success in life is to be of *'clean heart!*

This thought is boldly engraved in your ♥ heart ♥ in your ♥ mind ♥ in your ♥ body ♥ in your ♥ soul ♥ and in your ♥ spirit ♥. Just as your desire to seek me out, this thought, too, has always been written in your very DNA as part of your *'energynetic code'*™. You are forever infused, with this divine *Tri-essence Vibration*™. It is truly divine, for it comes from the Great Light, the Great Source of All --- It comes from Spirit."

Jaren listened to the Wise Lady with great respect and admiration and felt an overwhelming sense of gratitude to have learned so much, and to be in the presence of one so gifted and self-assured, yet so humble.

And now, before we can proceed with the specific steps of your apprenticeship as *Keeper of 'The Clean Heart Grid'*®, the time has come to address the issue which, on the surface, inspired you to come to me in the first place. Spirit instilled within you a specific purpose in your mind contained in your *'energynetic code'*™ to be the best you could be in your chosen field. You see, every guardian in our lineage unknowingly seeks to be the best he or she can be. Even our respective mastery of a skill is a precious gift from Spirit. For example, as you know, Dear One, I am merely a vessel of Spirit in transferring my expertise to you. And my wisdom and gifts in this area are always secondary to *The Tri-essence Vibration*™, as are yours.

THE SECRET OF THE *'CLEAN HEART GRID'*®

Jaren remained quiet, his eyes full of passion, his mind enthralled by all that he had heard and he was eager to hear more.

"Are you ready, Dear One, to address the matter of your performance enhancement? In order to take over as guardian of the sacred *'Clean Heart Grid'*®, you must manifest mastery of your chosen life skill. This is a vital task for each and every guardian of the sacred *Grid*," she noted, without really needing a verbal response to her question.

"I know that you already know my answer," he said with a reverent chuckle. "Besides, you are reading my heart every second, aren't you, dear *Mind Coach*®?"

The caring *Mind Coach*® smiled sweetly back at Jaren with a charming little wink in his direction to acknowledge his reaction.

"I know that you can see right through me and your sweet smile and charming wink have just confirmed that," remarked Jaren as a rosy blush colored his sweet face. "And yet, I still feel so comfortable in your presence. I know that it is your kind and loving energy, full of wisdom, which you are constantly directing at me that puts me so at ease. Thank you for all of it...I hope that I will learn to do the same, dear *Mind Coach*®!"

"You already do. I am simply teaching you the refinements of the process," she responded.

"Alas…Alas," continued the *Mind Coach*®. "There are so many learnings and may today be the first among many days of wonderfully exhilarating instruction. First, in order to be of assistance in your personal growth and performance enhancement, you must answer the following question: 'What is your greatest desire in the context of performance? I know that you will be totally honest with yourself."

Jaren thought for a minute and replied:

"Hmm….To….To become the best that I can be both personally as a human being and professionally as a performer in my field, and to prove it by winning in the *Great Games*."

"*Ena Binati*. Take heed, Dear One. *Ena Binati*.", she reiterated with her usual, reassuring look of wisdom.

"As I have already told you, merely winning is not the true measure of success. Just to compete in the *Great Games* is to win. And more important, as future *Keeper of 'The Clean Heart Grid'*®, it

THE SECRET OF THE *'CLEAN HEART GRID'*®

is your duty, Jaren, of the powerful and distinguished *House of Jenari*, to be more than a great performer. It is your duty to elevate yourself to a still higher level --- to that of *Elite Performer*, *Elite* in the sense of *Noble*. It is your duty to nobly and admirably display and develop your talents as the reflection of the wonderful gifts of the Universe that are bestowed upon you by the Great Source of All, Spirit. Moreover, as future *Keeper of 'The Clean Heart Grid'*®, it is your duty to succeed and to be a wonderful role model for others to follow. And, it is through Spirit that I am here to teach you how to perform your duty and to use that gift wisely. Through Spirit, I am here to teach you how to beautifully mesh *The Tri-essence Vibration*™ with my *Magic Formulas*, customized for you alone."

THE STORY OF JAREN:
KEEPER OF THE 'CLEAN HEART GRID'®

CHAPTER II

THE LAWS OF ELITE PERFORMANCE™

The *Mind Coach*® stared at Jaren for a moment with an astute look in her eyes and then asked:

"In addition to the unconscious driving power of your *energynetic code*™, *WHY* do you consciously want to be the best that you can be by winning in the *Great Games*?"

Jaren hesitated a moment and then asked and responded to his own question.

"Do I need another reason? I guess I do."

"Yes," replied the *Mind Coach*®. "Remember your task as future *Keeper of the Grid* is to achieve mastery of your chosen field as an *Elite Performer*. And to become an *Elite Performer* and to succeed in the *Great Games*, you will have to train long and hard and to overcome many trials along the way. Mere training is not enough. To succeed in the *Great Games* and to succeed in your life Mission, you will need a powerful ally. That ally is your list of reasons! They are what keep you ever pointed on the road that leads to you accomplishing your goals. Many have turned back from the prize because they did not have powerful enough reasons to go forward. You can overcome any obstacle if you have a powerful *'WHY'*. Your powerful *'WHY'* is your greatest desire, a desire that is so strong that it becomes the very force behind both your conscious and unconscious thoughts and actions every moment of every day. Your *'WHY'*, Dear One, is all the more powerful because it is not ego driven."

"Dear *Mind Coach®*, while I am not vain, I do believe in myself and in my abilities," declared Jaren.

"That is different," explained the *Mind Coach®*. "You must believe in yourself so that you can achieve your goals and help others to do the same. Dear One, you embody a balanced self and later I will reveal the deeper meaning and importance of such balance. For now, always remember to say:

'I overcome any obstacle with my powerful '*WHY*'.'

--- Remind yourself of this daily," emphasized the *Mind Coach*®.

"I must write down this mini *mantrum* to recite every day. Is that all I need to succeed?" asked Jaren.

With a maternal gaze, the wise *Mind Coach*® stood silently for several minutes before responding.

"You must also have a technical coach. I am your *Mind Coach*® and my responsibility entails much more than these words imply, for I work with your ♥ mind ♥ as well as with your ♥ emotions ♥ your ♥ body ♥ your ♥ soul ♥ and your ♥ spirit ♥. That is still only part of the picture when it comes to performance. A technical coach can teach you, step by step, how to perform precisely your selected skill. Likewise in any job or any life situation, one more skilled than you will be able to teach you, step by step, how to perform precisely your selected skill. Do you listen to your technical coach?" she inquired.

"Yes," Jaren replied.

THE STORY OF JAREN:
KEEPER OF THE 'CLEAN HEART GRID'®

"In fact, when I told him about the work of the legendary *Mind Coach®*, he encouraged me to come to you."

"I am certain that he has guided you very well in his way," said the Wise Lady. "You must do what he tells you. Dear One, I cannot help you any further with performance enhancement unless you have learned to follow instructions and then to apply what you have been taught."

Jaren summoned up some courage, and asked further: "What else do I need?"

"Alas…Alas! Once you have that burning desire firing up your very soul, only then, Dear One, can you be ready to learn my *Primary Magical Formula*. The other Formulas will follow at a later time. Do you even know the name of the first of the many Formulas, Dear One, that comprise my '*Mind Magic Technology*'™? The first one is called THE PERFORMANCE ENCHANTMENT FORMULA™," announced the *Mind Coach®*, with a tinge of mystery in her voice.

"I conjured up this wonderful Formula after many years of observing, questioning and studying experts from many different fields in the act of performing their tasks. In my eyes, merely to enhance performance is only half of the performance equation. You need to enchant as well with your own magical potion of clever maneuvers combined with a dynamic display of your *energynetic*™ *brilliance*. Only then will you arrive at what I call *The Balanced Performance Vibration*. What I mean is that your beautifully evolved vibration radiates out to all who witness you, raising their own vibrations, even if only for a few moments as you captivate them with your spellbinding moves. You see, Dear One, for those who are of *'clean heart,'* enhanced performance is only partially rewarding if it is not enchanting the lives of others in the process. Bringing joy to others is what the true nature of performance enhancement is all about. *Enchant and enhance at the same time!* So, I enable you to achieve glorious *Performance Enchantment*™! And just think of the joy that it brings you in return! Dear One, enjoy being the best you can be, while you bring enchantment to those who come to witness your talents. *Performance Enchantment*™! That's what I do. That's what the first of my Formulas, is all about."

"Hearing that bring chills up and down my spine," ecstatically revealed Jaren.

"Chills probably like those you sometimes experience in the midst of competition, and yet different from the chills you felt earlier today, right?"

"Dear *Mind Coach*®, how did you know that?" asked Jaren.

With a glowing smile on her face, the *Mind Coach*® answered Jaren and then began to lay out the important parts of *The Performance Enchantment Formula*™.

"With my help, these chills will serve as directed, personal messages to you. Enchanting, isn't it!?! And why not? My goal is to magically transform your competitions into enchanting performances! You will begin to mesmerize your audiences with your astounding abilities. You will totally captivate them with your inspired performances and I do mean inspired! For you, too, as an *Elite Performer* are merely a vessel of Spirit running through you!" exclaimed the *Mind Coach*®.

Jaren could not help but be himself mesmerized by her unique beaming radiance and by her soft, soothing voice, full of enthusiasm which calmed him and energized him at the same time.

THE LAWS OF ELITE PERFORMANCE™

"Dear One, you will eventually learn the rest of this puzzle from me as well," replied the *Mind Coach®*. "Right now, though, you must learn the nine specific components of my *Performance Enchantment Formula™*. *I have named them THE NINE MIND ENERGIES™*. These *Mind Energies™* form the mental foundation of *Elite Performance*; and each one carries within it a mental vibration that can be enhanced accordingly to achieve a particular mini goal along the way. Each *Mind Energy™* attracts what is needed to manifest realization of itself, as well as of the overall manifestation of your grand goal."

Jaren sat quietly listening to her every word.

"Few are those who have succeeded at incorporating all of *The Nine Mind Energies™* she went on to say.

"When I first began this work ages ago, no one had ever heard about these things. Now, as with all else in this land, information spreads faster than the speed of light. With this huge quantity of information, the quality becomes quickly tainted. Beware, therefore, Dear One, of contaminated information that can and will be misused in the wrong hands. *Ena Binati*. Take heed, Dear One.

THE STORY OF JAREN:
KEEPER OF THE 'CLEAN HEART GRID'®

Ena Binati," cautioned the *Mind Coach*® sternly as she continued.

"The *First* of *The Mind Energies*™ is *THE SUCCESS PLAN*, a critical ingredient too often neglected. It is no accident that *The Success Plan* is first because within it is contained the *nucleus energy* of each of the successive *Mind Energies*™. A Success Plan is your personal blueprint for the series of actions leading to your goal. All of the other *Mind Energies*™ must fit into this plan in order to create a self-contained mental energy system, the *synergynetic flow*™, that sets the stage for the unfolding of your plan. You need a *Success Plan* because the task of reaching your goal can only be accomplished by a repetition of small efforts. Furthermore, you need it because of one very important truth which is:

CHANCE FAVORS THE PREPARED MIND.

Remember this too: You need it because

THINGS ONLY BECOME BETTER BY CHANGE, AND NOT BY

CHANCE.

You need it because

FOR THINGS TO CHANGE YOU MUST CHANGE.

You need it because

THE LAWS OF ELITE PERFORMANCE™

EVEN THE LONGEST JOURNEY MUST BEGIN WITH A SINGLE STEP."

Jaren was taking it all in with a look of sheer joy and amazement. These potent words really hit home.

"Chance favors the prepared mind. Chance favors the prepared mind. Chance favors the prepared mind...!" recited Jaren aloud.

"Dear One, you are learning well and this, too, is no accident." responded the Mind Coach®.

Jaren thought for a moment and then asked:

"Wise Lady, what are the components of this *Success Plan*?"

The *Mind Coach*® gave him a profound look saying:

"Dear One, you need to know one very important thing. You need to know your destination in order to trigger the *nucleus energy* of all the other *Mind Energies*™. Once you know where you are going, you will need to know what steps you must take to get you there. You need to have both long term and short term goals. You need to know what short term goals will provide the stepping stones to the final stop along the way: winning in the *Great Games* or reaching whatever goal you want in life. Without these mini or short terms goals to guide you on your path to success, you will lack the specific and necessary vibrations to focus on the end result. Success is made easier when you take one step at a time. Figure out where you need to be one, two, three and four years before the *Great Games* or before any goal you seek to attain in your life. Decide at which tournaments, at which competitions, at what life points it is important to peak. Decide where you would like to be at specific points in your life and plan accordingly."

Jaren stood with his mouth open and then asked another question.

"Kind and Wise Lady. What you are saying is perfectly clear to me. I've always had goals, yet I never made the distinctions you now lay out before me. And I had never known how to change before, nor had I thought about creating the necessary vibrations to change, until now. What else do I need to do?"

The *Mind Coach*® was delighted to see his enthusiasm and continued to respond in her serene and melodious voice.

"Next, to outshine the others, you must incorporate *The*

Second Mind Energy™ of *The Performance Enchantment Formula™* into your entire being: you must have a *STRONG SENSE OF SELF*. This *Second Mind Energy™* is important in its own way, for it carries the vibrations of your identity. A mastery of this *Mind Energy™* allows you to reach a level of understanding of what makes you who you are. It allows you to acknowledge your strong points and your weak points. That means having the awareness to know what you need to improve upon to achieve confidence and technical perfection in order to sparkle. You must be aware of what techniques or refinements you need to learn, and be aware of which ones you need to improve."

"Be aware of what vibrations you need to release. If you are holding on to beliefs and emotions that get in the way of your success, then the time has come to let them go. And, of course, let go of them with great nobility of thought, feeling and action! Even those who are of *'clean heart'* may sometimes become angry or sad or upset. Such emotions are mired in *negavations™* and muddle our thoughts and actions. They obstruct self-confidence and poise. Let them loose forever into eternity, never to be seen again."

"I have tried to release some of these emotions and they still come back at times," said Jaren.

"To try to do something is the harbinger of defeat, Dear One. It represents half-hearted energy of thought and action. The result is to stand in the way of progress," responded the *Mind Coach®* in a decidedly emphatic tone of voice.

"Remember *THE PASSION OF DESIRE* for it is *THE THIRD MIND ENERGY*™ of *The Performance Enchantment Formula*™. The intensity of desire is a potent vibration, capable of withstanding almost any impediment that may get in the way. Make sure that it is a genuine desire that is not harmful to anyone or anything. A desire that is detrimental to the health and well being of another is a severe violation of Cosmic Law! Also, when you truly desire something, it is not tempered with hesitation. Desire does not translate into trying. Desire means doing. When you desire something with great passion and with a positive intention that reflects Divine Will, every cell of your being is imbued with an enhancing vibration that keeps you motivated to transform that desire into a reality. The more intense the desire, the stronger the resulting vibration that leads to manifestation of the desire."

"Dear *Mind Coach®*, you of all people know how much I want to perform beautifully each and every time, and that my desire to shine overwhelms me at times. It is only because I am so anxious to succeed that I sometimes lose perspective and do too much at once," replied Jaren with a sigh.

"Learning how to release unwanted thoughts and feelings plays a huge role in *Elite Performance*, and before I can teach you these processes, you must master *THE FOURTH MIND ENERGY™* of *The Performance Enchantment Formula™*: *PATIENCE AND CONSOLIDATION*. You must assimilate these two vibrations into the learning process and in relation to what I am teaching you. You must learn *Patience* because I am telling you things when they are meant to be revealed --- not a second before, not a second after. You must acquire *Patience of Learning*. Each parcel of knowledge is given when deemed appropriate. You listen, you absorb, you assimilate and you act upon what you learn. You *Consolidate* each parcel and then learn more, *wíla, willà*."

THE STORY OF JAREN:
KEEPER OF THE 'CLEAN HEART GRID'®

"I know that I probably have a puzzled look on my face whenever I hear these strange words that you use," asserted Jaren in a curious tone of voice.

"I know that occasionally I use words that are totally unfamiliar to you." remarked the *Mind Coach*®. "This one, *wíla, willà*, is *Jenari* code language for '*etcetera*' and carries a specific power within it. I will teach you many more of these powerful words and their significance later on during your apprenticeship as you follow, of course, a specific rhythm of *Learning* and then *Consolidation*, followed by more *Learning* and more *Consolidation*, in sequence. For example, when you assimilate each *Mind Energy*™ of my *Performance Enchantment Formula*™, you incorporate one vibration at a time as you are learning about it, then *Consolidate and Learn* about the next one. This creates a smooth, energetic flow at each level of your being, the *synergynetic flow*™. You will understand this better in a short while. You also, Dear One, need *Patience* when performing something new. It may require more time than you wish to incorporate a new thing, so you need to practice *Patience*," explained the *Mind Coach*®.

THE LAWS OF ELITE PERFORMANCE™

"Wise Lady, please tell me more!" asked Jaren.

"Is that showing patience?" she responded in an amused tone of voice. *THE FIFTH MIND ENERGY*™ of *The Performance Enchantment Formula*™ is to *EXPECT THE UNEXPECTED.* When you adopt this mind set, what you are doing is attracting the energies needed to support you when and if something occurs outside of your control. Dear One, you came to see me with an open mind and heart, not knowing what to expect, so the nucleus energy of this mind set is already in place. An *Elite Performer* must be open minded to new possibilities of action. An *Elite Performer* must anticipate in advance any adversity and prepare for it long before it arises. You may be the best planner in the world and still an unforeseeable challenge may arise. So, when an emergency pops up, it is not the time to be figuring out what to do about it. *Expect the Unexpected.* Dear One, when faced with adversity, when faced with an unexpected challenge, an *Elite Performer* remains self assured, stabilized by the vibration of preparedness that permeates his being. He or she is prepared with impenetrable mental resilience, with boundless strength of spirit and with immense physical endurance. You have two choices before you: Under the stress of competition, you can either take control and perform superhuman tasks or else you can fall apart and be a victim of circumstances. Which will you choose, Dear One?" asked the *Mind Coach®*.

"I choose the former!" asserted Jaren. I can now see that in the past when I faltered, it was because I was not prepared for unexpected situations."

"Precisely," responded the *Mind Coach®*. "The choice you make is a result of proper training. You need to have anticipated the emergency ahead of time and have carefully rehearsed what to do, before it happens. And, of course, you need to practice, practice, practice. Only perfect practice makes perfect. *Ena Binati*, Take heed, Dear One. *Ena Binati*. Beware, however, of too much practice, lest you exhaust your body, your mind and your spirit. Contrary to popular belief, practice does not make perfect. Only perfect practice makes perfect. Having your plan provides the framework of energies from which to draw to facilitate your ability to deal with unexpected situations. A *Success Plan* is not enough, however. You will also need another plan, which is *THE SIXTH MIND ENERGY*™ *of The Performance Enchantment Formula*™: you need to have a *Conditioning Plan*. You must develop both a mental and a physical conditioning plan in order to achieve the level of *Elite Performance*. Such a plan will enable you to get into what I call your *Maximum Performance State*™. Your *MPS*™, for short, contains the compact configuration of vibrational patterns which raise performance to superior levels. *Decoding* each person's unique Master Pattern to achieve *Elite Performance* has been an intriguing journey for me over the years. I will come back to this later on."

Jaren looked at the Wise Lady out of the corner of his eye and asked: "Dear *Mind Coach*®, what do I have to do to get into my *Maximum Performance State*™?"

The *Mind Coach*® grinned with a pleased look on her face.

"You assimilate The *SEVENTH MIND ENERGY*™ *of The Performance Enchantment Formula*™. *Number Seven is perhaps one of the most important secrets you will learn in your entire life, for it is a direct reflection of a Major Truth of the Universe,"* proclaimed the Wise Lady. "Dear One, this secret lies at the basis of all that you will ever do or, perhaps more important, not do, for that matter. It is the secret to living life itself! This secret is the following: Your mind, body, soul and spirit are connected as one and the same in a single vibrational *synergynetic flow*™. And each one effects the other in one, continuous *synergynetic flow*™. You must be able to control all of them at will, and learning how to do so is the basis of *The Seventh Mind Energy*™ of *The Performance Enchantment Formula*™.

As she uttered these words, the *Mind Coach*® began to make back and forth, spherical like gestures and proceeded on.

"One continuous flow," she said, continuing to gesture in this manner as she spoke. So close your eyes. Take a gentle, deep breath and listen. *Ena Binati.* Take heed, Dear One. *Ena Binati.*"

The *Mind Coach*® raised her hands together in a series of mysterious circular movements and began to speak again in a curious tongue.

Nemoishti. Dear one, you have a great power within you, a vibration so strong that you must learn to control this power. For if you do not, this great power within you will control you utterly every moment of every day. It will make you do things that you do not want to do. It will make you a victim of its whims; and most of all, it will make you fail. So how do you take charge of this inner power? You take charge of this inner power by training your mind, your body, your will, your emotions and your spirit. The key is to understand a simple *Great Truth of Being*. It is that your ♥ mind ♥ body ♥ soul ♥ spirit ♥ connection is a powerful force that lies at the very center of your being. Moreover, it is a powerful force that you can control, if you so choose. As with all else, the choice is yours."

With some hesitation in his voice, Jaren chimed in.

"From what I have learned from you thus far, I see that all of life is a choice. I always want to make the right choices that will make me better in every way. You know, that feeling I have inside a lot is telling me that there is no choice but one for me."

"Indeed. Indeed. Indeed," replied the *Mind Coach*®. You are learning well, Dear One. Now I ask you to assimilate *The Corollary of the Great Truth of Being* which is: Your ♥ mind ♥ body ♥ soul ♥ spirit ♥ connection will always do what you tell it to do! So you need to create the appropriate vibrational patterns to nourish and guide this *synergynetic flow™*. You do so by learning how to open the proper channels of communication with each of them. Of course, so few souls are aware of this; and I know that they are not meant to know at this point in time in their path. YOU, Dear One, are destined to know this, however. It is crucial that you pay attention to the vibrational patterns you create by what you are telling your ♥ mind ♥ body ♥ soul ♥ spirit ♥ connection. Moreover, it is critical that you tell this connection what you want in a way that is meaningful. Be vigilant every second of every day and create the perfect vibrational pattern for your mind ♥ body ♥ soul ♥ spirit ♥ connection in all that you do!"

"Dear *Mind Coach*®, how do I tell it what it needs to hear?" asked the anxious Jaren.

"I will tell you what it needs to hear. Begin now, Dear One. Close your eyes. Take another deep breath. Inhale deeply and exhale gently in nine increments. Feel a soothing calm coming over you. Relax. Let go of any tension and open your ♥ mind ♥ body ♥ soul ♥ spirit ♥ to the words now spoken. 'Imagine, can't you, a large movie screen in your mind!?! Beautiful...now, won't you make a large, bright, clear, sharp movie in your mind of yourself performing your skill perfectly, whatever it is. Don't you look wonderful accomplishing your task so flawlessly! Then like magic, take a wondrous step inside your personal movie and experience what it feels like. Feel the *posivations™*! Doesn't this picture feel incredibly sublime!?! Take notice that the pictorial pattern created, for it retains the very vibrations you require for *Elite Performance*."

Before the *Mind Coach®* could continue, Jaren reluctantly and politely interrupted.

"Wise Lady, I am sorry to interrupt, but I have a question, please."

"Before you ask your question, I have a command of you!" the *Mind Coach®* declared in a rather imposing tone of voice, while raising her right arm and pointing her index finger toward the sky.

"From this day forth, I command you to banish the word 'but' from your vocabulary. If any time you utter the word by mistake, you will immediately sense an inner warning signal to stop. From this day forth, the word 'AND' shall replace 'but'. The word 'AND' creates a smooth flow of the ♥ mind ♥ body ♥ thought ♥ action ♥ process and it facilitates the execution of the task performed."

Jaren rephrased his previous statement.

"I am sorry to interrupt, AND I have a question, please," he repeated. "That already feels better inside! It's like a block has been removed from me!"

"Oh really," she laughed in her soft manner. Quite precisely! You are literally taking away the obstruction created on a subconscious level! So what is your question, Dear One?" she asked.

"Dear *Mind Coach*®, I've come to realize that everything that you say and do is no accident. So why are you asking me to exhale in nine increments?" he pondered aloud.

"*Nine* is a magical number of great power in many ancient cultures, as well as in our present day. The number *Nine* is said to hold propitious vibrations. In other words, when exercised with a positive intention, the number *Nine i*s said to bring blessings and good fortune. Even more important, *Nine* represents 3x3, double the Trinity Blessing, the quintessential sacred vibration of the entire

Universe, carrying within it 3x3, or nine times the power to realize the intention. Also, notice the symbol I am wearing for '*The Clean Heart Grid*'®. It represents *The Tri-essence Vibration*™. Each side of the triangle represents one golden cord of *The Tri-essence Vibration*™, as RESPECT, INTEGRITY and DIGNITY, all of which energize the core of a '*clean heart.*' Dear One, I will tell you more about this symbol the next time we meet," asserted the *Mind Coach*®.

"I can see now that it is no accident either that you have that very symbol of '*The Clean Heart Grid*'® around your neck in gold and that I have...." he began to say.

The *Mind Coach*® chuckled again with an amused look on her face and continued his sentence.

"...and that you have a triangle on your shirt which is only part of the symbol. An accident, Dear One? Of course not, for there are no coincidences in this world. For you still have much more to learn. And all of this is another confirmation that your '*clean heart*' with its *Tri-essence Vibration*™ of the powerful and distinguished *House of Jenari*, is the real force which propelled you to work with me!" she proclaimed.

"Oh, kind *Mind Coach*®. It's all coming together in ways I had never imagined on many levels. I'm so excited!" Jaren joyfully shouted out.

"Speaking of imagining," the Wise Lady continued, "there are still other ways in which to control the vibrational patterns which enter your mind. Be constantly aware of the pictures in your mind. Push out all undesirable pictures that carry *negavations*™ and replace them with *posivation*™-laden images of what you want, of exactly what you want. Put all pictures of incorrect performance out of each level of your being. And remember that the Great Light of Spirit will not support any images of things that carry harmful vibrations to you or to others or to other things. Spirit, the Great Light of the Universe, will not allow any thought to manifest that is tarnished or any thought vibration that is not for the good of all! Cosmic Law demands such, and on this you can be certain!" she decreed.

"Now I understand why people with *negavations*™ get annoyed at me when I refuse to engage in rather unenlightened activities." Jaren reflected.

"The reason," she continued, "is that whether it be out of self-centeredness or anger, bitterness or dishonesty, these negative traits simply bring down their own vibration to an even lower level and intensify the initial *negavation*™. Dear One, remember that everything in the Universe is vibration, everything! Even your emotions! The more in touch you become with this simple, basic Truth, the easier it will become to grow and evolve to a higher level of being. You will find that those who carry negativity around them have a very hard time dealing with kindness directed towards them. They usually do not know how to respond to it."

"Dear One, there is still more. In order to control your mind, you must also pay attention to the vibrational patterns created by the voices in your head! Be aware of any voices that indicate negativity, such as fear or self doubt or what I call *'ego-drives.'* *'Ego-drives'* contain high levels of negative vibration. Remember that negative emotions such as these each carry a distinctive *negavation*™. Replace them with a voice telling you that you are succeeding. Banish these mental vampires from your mind, for they will drain your self confidence and will deprive you of your very spirit, your vital life energy--- your sustaining identity, so that you become a walking zombie of sorts, incapable of free will!"

"Dear One, you also need to pay attention to your body. Relax and release any tension. Release any negative feelings which house vibrations of fear or anxiety or self doubt. Feel a feeling of strength and determination. There is a narrow range in which your body responds most powerfully."

"All that is happening in my ♥ mind ♥ body ♥ soul ♥ spirit ♥ and I haven't been aware of it!" exclaimed Jaren.

"Are you aware of your heartbeat, Dear One?" asked the *Mind Coach*®.

"I'm sure that it's not in the way that you are going to explain," responded Jaren.

"For example, your heart must not beat too fast or too slow. Your breathing must not be too fast or too slow. Everything has to be 'just right' and in balance. I will soon teach you the deeper meaning of balance. Now you must discover what 'just right' is for you and learn how to get your body there whenever you perform. I will continue to work with you in other meetings, to help you get your *'just right'* just right for you and only you. This *'just right'* activates your *MPS™* when you need to be in that special vibrational pattern to attain *Elite Performance*. I have been blessed to work with so many wonderful beings from different fields of endeavor. Spirit, the Great Light of the Universe, has given me the wisdom and experience to differentiate the scores of *'just right'* feelings and distinctive vibrational patterns among them all, so that I may transfer that knowledge to all these wonderful beings," replied the *Mind Coach®* and continued on without a pause.

"Although I have merely touched upon ways in which to control the ♥ mind ♥ body ♥ soul ♥ spirit ♥, it is enough for you to understand *The EIGHTH MIND ENERGY™* of my *Performance Enchantment Formula™: MASTERING THE MOMENT.* That is what I have named this critical *Mind Energy™*. You must be able to stay focused in 'the present moment'. If you miss the mark of *Mastering the Moment,* you will unconsciously trap yourself in past mistakes and failures. *Elite Performers* are capable of elegantly capturing 'the now,' 'the present moment'! In short, they maintain razor sharp focus of the task at hand. You see, Dear One, *Elite Performers* have the keen ability to stay focused under the pressures of competition or any anxiety-laden situation primarily because they stay in *'the now.'* They master all that is happening around them to bring their focus inside, within themselves. This clears the way for enhancing *posivations*™ to support the smooth flow of perfect execution of the task. If something goes askew, they immediately put the *negavations*™ attached to the incident behind them, and quickly and sharply focus their awareness on the task at hand in *'the present moment.'* They accomplish this brilliant maneuver by using the patterns of *The Seventh Mind Energy*™ to control effortlessly the ♥ mind ♥ emotions ♥ body ♥ and ♥ spirit ♥ as one graceful and interconnected flow."

"Finally, Dear One, now that you have developed a *Success Plan* and have laid out the steps of your journey to your destination, now that you have cultivated a *Strong Sense of Self,* now that you have kindled within that *Burning Desire* to succeed on every level of your being, now that you have practiced *Patience and Consolidation of Learning*, now that you have adopted the *Expect the Unexpected* mind set, now that you have produced a *Conditioning Plan*, now that you have learned the basics of how to Control the ♥ mind ♥ body ♥ soul ♥ spirit ♥, now that you have learned the importance of Staying in *'the present moment,'* you are ready to assimilate *THE NINTH MIND ENERGY™* of *The Performance Enchantment Formula™*: THE CREATION OF *THE PERFECT PERFORMANCE MANIFESTATION™*! Just as *The First Mind Energy™* incorporates all of the other *Eight Mind Energies™*, so does the *Ninth One*, although from a different perspective. *The Ninth Mind Energy™* is the energetic reflection of *Mind Energy™ One* in reverse, as though you were looking at an image reflected in a mirror. *The Ninth Mind Energy™* contains more than the nucleus vibrations of the other *Eight*. It possesses the completed vibrational patterns for each of the other *Eight Mind Energies™*, each one fully realized as itself. Dear One, you have within you the power to create your *Perfect Performance Manifestation™* when you focus on *Mind Energy™ Nine*."

"Once again, *Nine* is the powerful force behind the scene!" interjected Jaren.

THE STORY OF JAREN:
KEEPER OF THE 'CLEAN HEART GRID'®

"Yes, Dear One! Yes! Always remember the unique power and significance of the number *Nine*. You have taken one step at a time in your assimilation of each *Mind Energy*™, and in so doing, you are already attracting the vibrations in the Universe you need to achieve your grand goal. I have been showing you how to enhance the mental vibration which is sustained in each component of the *Formula*. As soon as you began laying out your plan with me, the nucleus of each *Mind Energy*™ already began attracting what was needed to manifest itself in order to engender the overall manifestation that is your grand goal," summarized the Wise Lady as she continued.

"You now have all the vibrational patterns you need to literally program the precise living picture image of your great desire onto your personal movie screen in your mind. You imprint the exact image using what I have taught you thus far, creating in full glory, the exciting sights, sounds, feelings and thoughts that accompany you in the realization of your dream in all of your bodies. As you perfect this picture, I will teach you more refinements." The *Mind Coach*® continued to speak without a break.

THE LAWS OF ELITE PERFORMANCE™

The miraculous creation of your *Perfect Performance Manifestation*™ lies within your very ♥ mind ♥ body ♥ soul ♥ spirit ♥ connection! Finally, always be aware of what is happening in every aspect of your being. I cannot emphasize this enough! *Ena Binati.* Take heed, Dear One. *Ena Binati. Remember that your unconscious mind is continuously recording every single thought and sensation and image going through you, even if that thought or sensation or image lasted just a second. After all, everything is vibration! Everything!* Even our mental musings so that short, passing thoughts as well as profound ponderings hold the powerful potential of realization in this dimension. Every thought vibration is eternal, even if that thought is forgotten on a conscious level. *Ena Binati.* Take heed, Dear One. *Ena Binati, for whatever visual image you create in your mind, whatever you say to yourself and whatever you feel or think, consciously or unconsciously at any given point in time, carry the vibration for eventual manifestation as a present reality.* I will come back to this notion later. For now, though, take my advice: Monitor your mind. Monitor your mind. Monitor your mind."

THE STORY OF JAREN:
KEEPER OF THE 'CLEAN HEART GRID'®

"How do I do all of these things?" Jaren asked.

"Dear One, have you forgotten? They must be part of your overall plan. One step at a time in your journey. You must practice them continuously. And be aware of your thoughts and feelings and pictures. Monitor your mind!" she reiterated.

"Is there anything else I must do?" Jaren asked.

"Alas...Dear One. Indeed. The next time we meet I will teach you many refinements regarding *The Mind Energies*™. There is so much more. For now, though, rejoice, reward yourself and reach out to see, hear and feel the wonder and awe of your *Perfect Performance Manifestation*™ as a present, living reality of your beautiful dream. All of these powers have always resided within you, Dear One. I have simply revealed how to access them at will," responded the *Mind Coach*® with an endearing smile.

CHAPTER III

THE DIVINE NINE LAWS OF STAR PERFORMANCE™

The Wise Lady paused for a moment, staring at Jaren with beams of kindness streaming out from her entire aura. Then with a glimmer in her eye, she began presenting the next level of her wisdom:

"Dear One, I am still not done for the day. We have merely scratched the surface. You have acquired much, Dear One, about *The Divine Nine Mind Energies*™ and about their impact on performance. We will now move on to yet a higher level of *Performance Enchantment*™, to a level that is more magical than before and perhaps that is even more mystical, if I may say so! We now elevate our awareness and our very being to levels high above

THE STORY OF JAREN:
KEEPER OF THE 'CLEAN HEART GRID'®

in the sky --- *to the stars* --- high above the level of *Elite Performance* to the rarefied realm of....STELLAR PERFORMANCE!!! You already know that to shine far brighter than other good performers, you must be of *'clean heart.'* There are many performers in this land who have attained some level of success without being of *'clean heart.'* Yet, if they are not of *'clean heart,'* they cannot be elevated to this next level, to the level of the *Celestial Jewels* --- to the brilliant stars --- to become shining *Star Performers*! A *Star Performer* is like a rare gem, difficult to find and almost impossible to reproduce. Like a rare gem, a *Star Performer* displays countless facets of brilliance and reflects an almost regal quality in his or her performances. A *Star Performer* has triumphs of a noble nature, not based on vanity. A *Star Performer* has learned to become a master of all that is good, in spite of, rather than because of his or her skills. In short, a *Star Performer* embodies *The Tri-essence Vibration*™ which is further enhanced and ennobled to an enlightened state of being, beyond that of Elite Performer. A precious and powerful configuration of additional vibrations activates a potent vibrational convergence center, resulting in immediate transformation to a higher level of being. I will soon reveal to you the precise mechanisms at work in this vibrational convergence center. First, though, I will remind you once again, Dear One, of an essential Truth: Everything in the Universe is vibration --- everything --- all things animate and inanimate, things visible as well as invisible to the physical eye. Keep this in mind during the course of our next interaction. Remember too, that Spirit resides in your ♥ mind ♥ body ♥ and ♥ soul ♥; and when you clear the way for the Light of Spirit to shine within you without obstruction, everything is possible. Everything!"

The *Mind Coach®* proceeded with her most intense gaze thus far.

"Jaren, of the powerful and distinguished *House of Jenari*, there are Nine Mystical Laws to assimilate in order to reach the lofty level of *Star Performer*."

"I should have known that there would be *Nine* of them, right?" retorted Jaren in a teasing voice.

The eyes of the *Mind Coach®* sparkled with joy.

"Indeed, Dear One. You are learning and consolidating well.

THE STORY OF JAREN:
KEEPER OF THE 'CLEAN HEART GRID'®

You have come far and are truly ready for the next series of Formulas from my *Mind Magic Technology™*. These formulas represent the set of vibrational patterns which carry the Supreme vibrations of the entire Universe. I have named them *THE DIVINE NINE LAWS OF STAR PERFORMANCE™*, known as *THE DIVINE NINE™* for short."

"The First of *The Divine Nine Laws™* is the all encompassing *LAW OF TIMING* to which I have alluded time and time again. *Star Performers* know that there is a time and a place for everything that occurs in the Universe. Star Performers, therefore, choose their time and place. *Star Performers* use their *inner knowing* to choose the right time and the right place for them. *Star Performers* will never act before it is time to do so. Their *inner knowing* has shown them on numerous occasions, that haste really does make waste because everything happens for a reason. Each event and situation that occurs in our lives happens when it is supposed to happen, not a second before, not a second after. In fact, *Star Performers* will wait for the time to be right before proceeding, even if others perceive their reluctance to be indecision. One simply does not rush the Universe! Cosmic Law will not permit it!"

At this point before proceeding, the *Mind Coach*® placed her cupped hands at her heart center as she looked up with a beautiful glow on her face that joyously and graciously acknowledged Spirit.

"*Star Performers* know when to make their move because in their ♥ hearts ♥ in their ♥ minds ♥ in their ♥ bodies ♥ in their ♥ souls and in their ♥ spirits ♥, they know without question that there are no accidents, no coincidences in the Universe, only *Divine Timing.* Some call it *synchronicity.* It is *Divine Timing,* pure and simple. *Star Performers* know on some level within, that our notion of linear time is nonexistent for Spirit. We may desire immediate manifestation of something yet for Spirit, the notion of immediate is a moot one, since past, present and future are all one and the same for Spirit. *Star Performers* are aware of this distinction and live it out every moment of every day. I will reveal more to you regarding this notion later."

This time, it was Jaren who gave the Wise Lady a wink of recognition as he spoke:

"Oh, Wise Lady, when the time is right! At this moment I am in such awe of the workings of the Universe, that I have no words to describe what I am feeling in human terms! That warm quivering sensation is intensifying even more!"

The *Mind Coach®* responded with her cupped hands this time above her head for a few minutes.

"Dear One, the workings of Spirit follow the perfect rhythm of the Cosmos. The sound of the harp you are hearing is the celestial sign for the synchronistic significance of our meeting. *Synchronicity* is part of the flow of which I constantly speak. Dear One, know that the timing of our first encounter is literally and figuratively written in the stars. *Divine Timing*, pure and simple. Keep this thought in your conscious awareness as I continue to speak."

"Now, on to *The SECOND LAW,* which is just as important as the *First* one. It is *THE LAW OF SIMPLICITY*", declared the Wise Lady as she placed her hands at her *Heart Center* before resuming. "*Star Performers* seek simplicity in all that they do. They release all vibrations whether in thought, feeling or action that may complicate their journey to the final destination of achieving their goal. They let go of all *negavations*™, whether in the form of useless thoughts and emotions, pessimistic pictures in their head, inappropriate situations or undesirable companions who dare take them off the noble path of their soul's mission. It serves no purpose to complicate the journey to one's much desired destination. The flow of *The Manifestation Vibration* is made smoother and easier when there is minimal or ideally no interference at all from needless, superfluous and unwarranted *negavations*™. When the channels within you are free for Spirit to flow freely, everything is possible...everything!"

"Thus, *Star Performers* eliminate any form of excess around them and seek simplicity in everything. Just think when two lights come together without obstruction, your inner light and the Great Light of Spirit, the merged light that results is all the brighter and shines the way to *The Perfect Manifestation.* Seek out the power of this merged Light and let it shine within you with great brilliance! *The Simplicity Vibration* acts like a power switch, and it is this *Simplicity Vibration* that facilitates manifestation and fulfillment by the Divine when the time is right, not a second before, not a second after."

THE STORY OF JAREN:
KEEPER OF THE 'CLEAN HEART GRID'®

"THIRD, is THE LAW OF HUMILITY. Star Performers are humbly balanced and carry within them the VIBRATION OF HUMILITY. Star Performers identify closely with the champion within, without the least tinge of arrogance or narcissism. In victory, they do not flaunt their prize to shame others, nor do they put themselves on a pedestal. In short, they are discreet and authentic. Most of all, although Star Performers outshine others with their prowess, they accept this success, as a reflection of the Great Light of Spirit running through them. Star Performers are willing to release ego to the winds, and to allow the true essence of their soul to breathe in its enchanting elixir. Star Performers allow this essence to permeate every cell of their being and burst its way into spellbinding performance."

"FOURTH is THE LAW OF CLARITY. Star Performers embody the PURITY VIBRATION in every cell of their being. They maintain a standard of purity of ♥ mind ♥ body ♥ soul ♥ and ♥ spirit ♥. Star Performers possess at all times clarity of thought, feeling and action. Only then, can Star Performers relax their synergynetic flow™ to focus on and Master 'the now'! Moreover, Star Performers are able at any time to clear their vibration of any interference that may hinder their performance. They keep their physical body pure, free of noxious substances, whether in drink, nourishment or diversion. *Star Performers* are deeply aware of the *negavations*™ permeating these substances and avoid their ingestion. *Star Performers* must be able to call upon their great resources deep within in order to abandon themselves to their *inner knowing* of what perfect performance is for them. With clarity filling every cell of their being, only then, will the powers that guide us allow the channels of the ♥ mind ♥ body ♥ soul ♥ spirit ♥ to flow freely, unobstructed in any way. In short, when *Star Performers* have purity of ♥ mind ♥ body ♥ soul ♥ spirit ♥, only then, are they in the flow of perfect performance and more important, in the flow of Ultimate Perfection, that of Spirit."

"Dear *Mind Coach*®, I want so much to stay *in the flow* of receiving all that you are teaching me; and I feel like there is so much, that it's overwhelming at times!" exclaimed Jaren with a sigh.

"Alas! Alas...Dear One. I am well aware that the Universe is passing a tremendous amount of wisdom through me to you. You must trust in the Universe as well as in yourself, for your unconscious mind is assimilating all that you need to know and more. *Trust is the key.* And how timely your comment is!" she chuckled.

"For *THE FIFTH LAW* is *THE LAW OF TRUST. Star Performers* feel the reassuring flow of *THE TRUST VIBRATION* moving through them, at all times. *Star Performers* trust in the Universe, and as such, experience infinite trust in themselves, enhancing the vibration whenever needed, especially when the going gets tough in competition. If *Star Performers* happen to stumble along the way, they immediately affirm their faith in Spirit and utmost trust in *Divine Timing,* that all will be fine and in accordance to Divine Will, in accordance to Cosmic Law. *Star Performers* implicitly trust that all which happens is the result of the vibrational patterns of their every thought, feeling and action in both their conscious and unconscious minds prior to this moment in time. *Star Performers* also trust in themselves to have the right thoughts for *Perfect Manifestation* of their desires. This inexplicable sense of *inner knowing* always guides them to appropriate action. It helps them to know when they have lost focus on their goals. Having this trust always guides them to make the right choices on the road to success. This knowledge makes them all the more vigilant; and with such an immense resource of trust in Spirit running through them, there is nothing to fear, absolutely nothing!"

The *Mind Coach®* glanced at Jaren to indicate the importance of listening to her in order to maintain the stream of wisdom from Spirit flowing through her at this time. One could even say that there was an additional glow radiating around her head in a spiraling motion once again.

"*SIXTH*, Dear One, is *THE LAW OF GRATITUDE*. *Star Performers* embrace *THE GRATITUDE VIBRATION* in all that they do. *Star Performers* throw vanity to the wind and express humble thanks to Spirit for their abilities. They realize that their talents are not really their own and that they are precious gifts from the Universe. *Star Performers* know that the brilliance they display in flawless performance is merely a reflection of the exquisite perfection of the Great Light of Spirit; and for this, they genuinely express their heartfelt indebtedness to the Universe. And *Star*

THE STORY OF JAREN:
KEEPER OF THE 'CLEAN HEART GRID'®

Performers are grateful to those who appreciate their skills because this brings others closer to *The Gratitude Vibration*. Without gratitude for that which is, success is never complete!"

"Dear *Mind Coach*®, I am so grateful to you for sharing your wisdom with me!" exclaimed Jaren with great joy.

"It is I who am grateful to be in the presence of your beautiful soul from the powerful and distinguished *House of Jenari*, YOU, Dear One, who are to take my place as *Keeper of 'The Clean Heart Grid'*®," smiled the Wise Lady, as she proceeded.

"*SEVENTH*, is *THE LAW OF HARMONIC CONVERGENCE* or *BALANCE*. *Star Performers* maintain constant vibrational balance of all of their bodies --- the mental, emotional, physical and spiritual bodies. They achieve what I call a *Harmonic Convergence* of the ♥ mind ♥ body ♥ soul ♥ and ♥ spirit ♥ vibrations of their being. Certain enlightened ones have talked about the *Harmonic Convergence* of earthly vibrations occurring at particular times on the planet. This notion to which I refer is different in that it represents the point of intersection of all vibrational patterns of one's being, including those of one's *energynetic code*™. It is, of course, no accident that *The Law of Harmonic Convergence™ is Law Number Seven,* for *Seven* is the spiritual number for the creation of the magnificent Universe, and is most assuredly reflected many times over in the microcosmic aspects of the grand macrocosm that is life itself in its multitude of forms. For example, the number *Seven* happens to be the basis of the harmonic scale in music, among many numerous other things as well."

"Excuse me, wise *Mind Coach®,* as I just realized that the lovely notes of the harp are probably a reminder to me, on some level, of this powerful spiritual number," asserted Jaren.

"Dear One, you are learning well. The harp sounds you hear reflect the entire musical scale. In a profound and mystical way, the sounds emanating from these chords create the vibrations necessary to trigger the *Harmonic Convergence Center.* For now, in the context of *Star Performance,* it suffices to know that this concentration of energies at one central point is what allows *Star Performers* to sustain a high vibrational level at all times. This magnificent convergence point to which I alluded earlier today, keeps the *synergenetic flow™* of the ♥ mind ♥ body ♥ soul ♥ spirit ♥

connection moving smoothly. In so doing, it creates a soothing state of overall balance. I refer to this vibrational convergence center as the *STILL POINT*. Store this notion in a special place in the treasure chest that is your *synergynetic*™ *connection*, Dear One, for I will come back to it many times. For now though, simply remember that this still point provides an oasis of inner peace that strengthens the ability to focus on the task at hand. With the strength of the *still point* as a secure and steady force, *Star Performers* do not fall prey to temptations that are designed to distract them or to lower their vibrations. This wonderful center of converging vibrations is so powerful that it creates a strong internal equilibrium for *Star Performers* that also casts waves of energy towards all those around them by virtue of its intensity. The *still point* serves, then, as a potent stabilizing influence for *Star Performers* that can balance the vibrations of all those within his or her energetic reach, especially in this land, where inner personal chaos can easily tilt the scales towards disorder. That is why balance is so important in our land at the present time. It will help to restore equilibrium in all people in the land."

THE DIVINE NINE LAWS OF STAR PERFORMANCE™

"*EIGHTH*, Dear One, is *THE LAW OF RESPONSIBILITY*. *Star Performers* incarnate *THE RESPONSIBILITY VIBRATION* in all aspects of their being. They are acutely aware of their responsibility to uphold *The Tri-essence Vibration™*. *Star Performers* know that they are meant to spread this beautiful vibration all across the land. *Star Performers* know that in the final analysis, no matter what their earthly victories are perceived to be, that they are ultimately accountable only to Spirit, and to nothing and to no one else. *Star Performers* instinctively maintain a high standard of behavior. Part of their responsibility is an awareness and acceptance of their soul's Mission which they feel in their sacred *still point* somewhere in their body. That point is different for everyone. The place they experience the *still point* is different for everyone. *Star Performers* feel an indescribable desire to actualize this responsibility by embarking on the directed Mission of their soul. The message may come in a different form for each person. Once *Star Performers* become aware of their own mission, they also take action to help others become aware of their own life missions. For every soul in this land has a specific Mission, all of equal worth in the eyes of

THE STORY OF JAREN:
KEEPER OF THE 'CLEAN HEART GRID'®

Spirit, even if different from each other."

At this point, the *Mind Coach*® cupped her hands at her heart once again, uttering a few indistinguishable words, and then proceeded on with that same intense gaze fixed upon Jaren.

"Finally, Dear One, there is *THE NINTH LAW*, and perhaps the most *Magical*. It is *THE LAW OF TIME COMPRESSION*™ or what I prefer to call *THE LAW OF TEMPORAL MAGIC*™. *The Law of Temporal Magic*™ refers to the uncanny ability to distort the experience of time as we know it. *Star Performers* can contextually trigger time distortion when necessary in order to perform a special task. *Star Performers* mysteriously carry within them *The Divine Vibration of Non-existent Time*, translated into human terms as condensed time, where present, past and future come together as one, single, simultaneous moment. When they need to, *Star Performers* achieve the superhuman task of miraculously compressing time. We live within a range of linear time in this land which has nothing to do with the notion of time in other dimensions. *Star Performers* performing within their still point have the ability to enigmatically bridge the time gap by means of this powerful *Ninth*

Vibration, albeit momentarily, between human time and Divine Time."

"For *Star Performers*, even an instant counts. *Star Performers* know that in the heat of competition, in the throes of everyday life, a second may be an eternity, an eternity that may decide the outcome, their outcome, their destination. *Star Performers* know not to waste a single instant for each moment contains the vibrations of past, present and future, all infused into one. They know that to perform their task in super human fashion, they need to perform a *Temporal Miracle™*. That *Temporal Miracle™* is the act of time compression, of time distortion. In fact, for *Star Performers* the notion of time as we know it disappears for all practical purposes. *Star Performers* make time magically vanish with their mystical, *vibrational magic wand* carried inside of them, much to the awe of those fortunate to witness this *Temporal Miracle™*."

"How do I perform such magic?" Jaren asked with excitement.

"I will gladly tell you," said the Wise Lady. First, Dear One, go and think about all that I have told you. As you review these learnings, remember that *The Divine Nine Laws of Star*

THE STORY OF JAREN:
KEEPER OF THE 'CLEAN HEART GRID'®

Performance™ also carry The Tri-essence Vibration™ of a 'clean heart.' Remember, too, that, in reviewing all that I have shared with you, that you will Learn and then Consolidate each parcel of wisdom. That is what I would like you to do right now, and then come back to see me tonight just before dark. Once you have done this, and not a second before, not a second after, I will tell you with great delight, how to create your own brand of Temporal Magic™."

So Jaren went away and spent several hours reviewing in his mind everything that the dear, wise Mind Coach® had told him, so he would remember. It was almost dark when Jaren returned to the enchanted place of the Wise Lady. An unusually bright, full moon illuminated the entire landscape with what appeared to be an unusual, glittery sheen.

"Ah! Dear One. I see that you have come for the final Divine Nine Law™," declared the Wise Lady.

After pausing a moment, she gazed up at the brilliant night sky and then cupped her hands at her Heart Center, reciting some other strange words. Suddenly, the sound of soft harp chords filled the air once again at which point the wise Mind Coach® gracefully moved her cupped hands, this time, to a position right above her head, uttering another strange phrase and then said:

"Dear One, this enchanting evening it is no accident that a luminous full moon lights up the sky above us, infusing the countryside with an almost magical glow. Nor is it a coincidence that we meet today, or that you are learning these secrets on the day and night of a full moon; for the moon on the date of its complete cycle radiates enhanced vibrations of power. The light of the moon on this night greatly empowers all undertakings and rituals of a mystical nature. A potent vibrational pattern is set up around the Earth at this time, a pattern which automatically links itself to any mystical act taking place anywhere on the planet. Furthermore, there is a profound connection between the full moon and '*The Clean Heart Grid*'® about which you will learn the next time we meet."

The *Mind Coach*® again gracefully raised her cupped hands to her heart, uttering a few more of her words unfamiliar to Jaren's ears and then proceeded.

"Dear One, '*clean heart*' that you are, tonight you seek to learn what else you need to do in order to create your own *Temporal Magic*™! And I say to you, Dear One, *Ena Binati. T*ake heed, Dear One. *Ena Binati,* for you must find your *inner vibrational magic wand* that will allow you to compress time. Remember what you learned with *The Nine Mind Energies*™ concerning focus. Access that parcel of wisdom. Feel that feeling of *inner knowing*! Then, take a gentle, deep breath. See and focus with your mind's eye on what I am saying. Focus your attention on the sound and on the touch of my voice. Feel my *Tri-essence Vibration*™ calling your name, Jaren, of the powerful and distinguished *House of Jenari*."

"Dear *Mind Coach®,* your voice seems to touch my very soul; and I'm actually feeling and hearing and seeing the warm quivers in my heart center! How awesome!"

Upon hearing these words, Jaren felt the warm quivers more intensely than every before as the Wise Lady continued.

"You know, don't you, Dear One, that time slows down when you can narrow your focus to only a very small area and ignore everything else around you. It is like looking through a narrow tunnel. And now I ask you, Jaren, of *Jenari* lineage, to perform a special ritual. Tonight, I would like you to go out in the open field and look up at the gorgeous night sky and find a star, not just any star. I would like you to gaze up at the myriad stars in the Heavens and find your own STAR, that one STAR that is YOURS and yours alone! Avoid haste in your search. Cup your hands together at your *Heart Center*, as I have shown you many times. Stay *'in the now'* and MASTER THE MOMENT!!! Won't you focus, now, Dear One, on *'the present moment'* and feel past and future meshing gloriously into it! Clear your mind. Relax. You will know when you have found your own star, for you will sense a vibration within heretofore unknown to you. There will be no doubt at all, in your ♥ mind ♥ body ♥ soul ♥ spirit ♥ connection, for you will be in that fortuitous flow which I call the *still point*. Remember this well for your *still point* is your *Center of Harmonic Convergence* of *The Divine Nine™ Vibrations*. Remember, you will be guided by your *inner knowing*.

"Dear One, feel that *inner magic wand* pointing upward to the *STAR* marked with your very essence. When you have found your personal *STAR*, FEEL *The Gratitude Vibration* becoming more intense within you; and express your heartfelt gratitude to the Universe for this precious gift. Experience and rejoice in the beautiful oneness of it all. Rejoice in your gift of oneness with the Universe! Then cup your hands together once again and place them at your *Heart Center* while you inhale quickly and exhale in nine increments, fixing your gaze on your beautiful *STAR*. Make your magic by asking all the powers Above and within you to come together at your *still point!* Focus and concentrate on your *STAR* in the sky with both your physical eyes and with your mind's eye simultaneously until all of the other stars disappear!

Do so with humbled awe and gracious gratitude. When you can do that, Dear One, you will master time! You will find an extraordinary inner tranquility fueling you with tremendous energy. It is an incredibly beautiful and liberating feeling, like none else you will ever experience. When you first master yourself and can compress time, you will be able to do all that you need to do in order to reach your goal, whatever that goal."

"Oh kind and wise Lady, I feel so incredibly wonderful, as though I am...in a different place... a different time! I am so appreciative of the wisdom that you have shared with me. I do not have the words to express the immense gratitude that is overflowing from within for all that you have done for me. Thank you! Thank you! Thank you, dear *Mind Coach®!* Nine times thank you! I am sure that as time goes on, I will be even more thankful as we work together during my apprenticeship to become the future *Keeper of 'The Clean Heart Grid'®.* I know that I will continue to consolidate the wisdom you are passing on to me. I do not know what to say or how to thank you!"

"Dear One, I am deeply touched by the purity of your being! I so honor you once again, Jaren, of the powerful and distinguished *House of Jenari,* by cupping my hands to my *Heart Center* as I bear witness to your *'clean heart'* and to the tears of joy streaming down your grateful face. Dear One, know that the joy of your metamorphosis is my great reward, for now you, too, *'clean heart'* that you are, Jaren of the powerful and distinguished *House of Jenari,* shall evolve to a higher level of being than ever before. And you shall bring tremendous joy to those blessed ones who will now cross your path."

THE STORY OF JAREN:
KEEPER OF THE 'CLEAN HEART GRID'®

Upon saying these words a mysterious, spiraling light appeared around her, at which point she turned so quickly, that she seemed to almost vanish into thin air! Only the distinct scent of fragrant carnations and camellias lingered sweetly in her place.

And with this sign, Jaren went out into the lush, open meadow not far from the place he had met with the Wise Lady beneath the great night sky. He felt somehow different inside. He knew that he had changed in a profound way. He now felt an incredible swirling of powers within of which he had been unaware until his meeting with the wise *Mind Coach*®. He had learned a great deal and in learning what he did, he acquired great wisdom about who he was and who he was yet to become, in ways he had never before imagined until his encounter with the wonderful *Mind Coach*®. He was truly in awe of life, of the great talent he was given and now, of the great wisdom he had received as well. Jaren knew in his heart with a great passion of desire, that he was ready to grow and become the beautiful person and great performer to which he had aspired. Jaren found the missing piece in ways he had not imagined before meeting the lovely Wise Lady. Now he felt whole.

And yet there is still more.

Jaren also knew now, that with the guidance of the *Mind Coach*®, he would be ready to take over his duty when the time was right, as *The Keeper of 'The Clean Heart Grid'*®. *He was deeply aware, that with this honor came a huge responsibility....the responsibility to uphold all that 'The Clean Heart Grid'*® *represents -- The Tri-Essence Vibration*™ qualities of RESPECT, INTEGRITY and DIGNITY. As soon as he had this thought, he was for the first time acutely aware of a very distinct, spiraling vibration moving through him. It made him comprehend on every level that this responsibility was even greater in another way, because as future *Keeper of 'The Clean Heart Grid'*®, Jaren is to be responsible for spreading *The Tri-Essence Vibration*™ throughout the land to as many people as he could.

"Dear Ones. Listen, NOW, to my words, won't you and be aware of the magnificent transformation occurring at this very moment among us, for the light of *'The Clean Heart Grid'*® in the sky above is shining its enhancing rays upon the ♥ body ♥ mind ♥ soul ♥ and ♥ spirit ♥ of each person in this land and beyond. Even

THE STORY OF JAREN:
KEEPER OF THE 'CLEAN HEART GRID'®

the unenlightened ones are beginning to receive, unknowingly, this beautiful, magnified light of transmutation. Whether they know it or not, the powerful rays emanating from *'The Clean Heart Grid'*® are radiating continuous beams of Love, just like the healing balls of Light from Spirit that I send to all. For the time is NOW, to receive the Great Blessing of the Universe, the miraculous gift of Spirit of exhilarating upliftment from the breath of the Divine. Be open to it, Dear Ones, and take in each atom and molecule as you take your every breath. Welcome it into every cell of your being, with my *Divine Nine Laws*™ as your personal guide."

And, yes, Jaren did find his *STAR,* that very special *STAR* that is his alone! He followed the instructions of the *Mind Coach*®. He gazed at his star more and more intensely until he suddenly realized that all of the other stars had miraculously vanished from the sky! A feeling of great joy and assurance came over him. He called upon the powers of Spirit to mesh beautifully with his point of *Harmonic Convergence.* The connection was like a spark of electricity igniting every cell of his being! Jaren felt a huge rush of energy swirling through his entire body. He felt an even more powerful force of several different vibrations coming together within him in his chest. Now he could identify this force, for it was his *STILL POINT*. The profound serenity of which the *Mind Coach*® had spoken overcame him. He was totally in *'the present moment,'* in the joyous now, having meshed with his *still point*, where present, past and future blend all into one! He saw only his star in his mind's eye and in front of his physical eyes. Suddenly, Jaren knew that he would have all of the time he needed to do what he had to do because TIME as he knew it had ceased to exist!

The *Mind Coach*® was right. It was as though time had disappeared! That night, much later, when he left the field, several people who saw him were struck by the intensity of his being which seemed to sparkle like a dazzling, white diamond. One even had a strange feeling that one had somehow witnessed the birth of a new *STAR*, for there was a special glow about Jaren, on this night, one they had not yet seen before...a glow similar to the one surrounding the lovely *Mind Coach*® and to that beautiful, glittery sheen radiating over the landscape from the light of the full moon on this very special night. The others had not seen this glow before

THE STORY OF JAREN:
KEEPER OF THE 'CLEAN HEART GRID'®

tonight, for they had witnessed a special something, for the very first time, as though they had been starstruck. They were no longer in the presence of a young, searching Jaren. A great change had occurred, and not by chance! No, not by chance, for Jaren had sought the wisdom of the *Mind Coach*®, and had mastered his life task, so that he could accept from Spirit, the precious gift of *Keeper of 'The Clean Heart Grid'®*. Jaren became better by changing the way he thinks about his thoughts. He became better by learning the customized *Mind Magic Formulas*™ of the Wise Lady. Jaren became better by learning *The Divine Nine Mind Energies*™ of her *Performance Enchantment Formula*™. He became better by learning *The Divine Nine Laws*™. In so doing, he raised his vibrations even more and continues to stand up for his high moral standards! And Jaren shines brightly now, for he found his *STAR* which is to light the way for those younger than he who are to follow in his footsteps, because this young person of *'clean heart'* had become *STAR PERFORMER*!!! Just as Divine Will had decreed, Jaren became a timeless *STAR* in his own right far outshining with his brilliance all those around him, thanks to the gifts of Spirit and to those of the wise *Mind Coach®....*

Jaren, of the powerful and distinguished *House of Jenari,* had passed the initial test required of every future *Keeper of 'The Clean Heart Grid'®* to prepare them for the grandiose guardianship awaiting them. He had elevated himself to the level of a truly, noble *STAR PERFORMER!* He was still anxious to learn more. He still wanted to learn the meaning of the *Mind Coach®'s* mysterious gestures, to learn the cryptic prayers she recited, to learn the mystery around the spiraling energy and light accompanying her, to learn how to detect different vibrations from afar and how to deal with them accordingly...and what about the full moon? Most of all, Jaren was anxious to learn how all of these things fit into *The Legend of 'The Clean Heart Grid'®.* Where did it come from? Who was the first Keeper of the sacred Grid? How was he or she chosen? Where will it shine its rays in the future? Whenever these thoughts came to mind, Jaren would remember the words of the wise *Mind Coach®:*

"Patience, Dear One, for everything that occurs is *Divine Timing,* pure and simple!"

THE STORY OF JAREN:
KEEPER OF THE 'CLEAN HEART GRID'®

Upon hearing these words, Jaren felt an overwhelming inner serenity, just like the first time he had laid his eyes upon the kind and Wise Lady. He could hear her words echoing over and over in his mind:

"Dear One, trust in yourself and in Spirit, for you, Jaren, of the powerful and distinguished *House of Jenari*, will learn all that you need to know about the fabulous *Legend of 'The Clean Heart Grid'®* when you are meant to do so, not a second before, not a second after. That will come next time when we meet again!"

NOW, why don't you, Dear Ones, listening to this story, join me, the *Mind Coach*® and the transformed young Jaren, the dazzling new *STAR,* on the next part of his journey as he etches out the sparkling facets of his soul's brilliant Mission. Join us, won't you, and learn the guarded secrets of the beautiful *Legend of 'The Clean Heart Grid'®.* Join us, won't you, and gain even more insights into the ancient wisdom of the ages when we meet again…

Meanwhile, Dear Ones, the next time you are out under the resplendent night sky, hear my words echoing in your mind; and take a peak at the scores of stars shining their light down upon you.

THE DIVINE NINE LAWS OF STAR PERFORMANCE™

Take the time to seek out your own *STAR* that is for YOU and YOU ALONE! For each of you has a *STAR*, a very special *STAR*, if only you knew how to find it; and NOW YOU DO! For when the time is right, not a second before, not a second after, each of you can be transformed into *STAR PERFORMER* of your chosen field with my guidance, within the framework of your own soul's Mission. Dear Ones, let me, the *Mind Coach*®, guide you to the discovery of your own true essence and to the joyous fulfillment of your soul's blessed mission. I therefore charge you with the following: Go out under the Heavens above and find your distinctive *STAR*! As you do this, remember my words echoing in your own mind:

True Success in life is not measured

by material gain...

True success in life is to be of '*clean heart*'!

When you do this, Dear Ones, a magnificent metamorphosis will occur! You will be mystically transported to another place, a miraculous place where time disappears. And if you are of '*clean heart*', suddenly, a great force of energy will swirl inside of you, bursting into the night sky, sparking the creation of your own *Celestial Jewel*, your personal *STAR* that will also shine throughout eternity....and when the time is right, you will learn about the beautiful *Legend of 'The Clean Heart Grid'®*, only then and not a second before, not a second after, because all is *Divine Timing*, after all. And you will discover your own *inner, vibrational magic wand*, your *Still Point*, and have your *STAR* become part of *'The Clean Heart Grid'®* which shines for all humanity and of which Jaren is the Sacred Keeper for now! Dear Ones, remember always:

SHINE AS THE BRILLIANT STAR THAT YOU ARE!

AND CARRY THIS THOUGHT THROUGHOUT ETERNITY...

ENA BINATI!

TAKE HEED...

DEAR ONES...

ENA BINATI!

SHINE AS THE BRILLIANT STAR THAT YOU ARE!!!

ABOUT THE AUTHOR

Marilyne Woodsmall, Ph.M. is a respected Behavioral Modeler, International Trainer/Consultant, *Mind Coach*®, Author, and expert in human typological research. For two plus decades she has synthesized her expertise and research in the areas of performance enhancement, entrepreneurship, learning and creativity, communication, leadership, management science, Neuro-Linguistic Programming (NLP), and cultural change.

Known as the *"Success Expert,"* she is one of the principals of *Advanced Behavioral Modeling™*, Inc., a consulting and training firm committed to increasing the performance and productivity of organizations and individuals using advanced behavioral science and learning technologies. She is the co-creator of *Advanced Behavioral Modeling™ Technology,* a behavioral science change technology for capturing, explicating, replicating and transferring expertise. Ms. Woodsmall has pioneered its development and application in numerous fields and has designed model-based trainings to increase and maintain high performance levels in high stress situations in private and corporate sectors and in athletic competition. The result: dramatically increased performance, reduced training time and slashed costs.

THE STORY OF JAREN:
KEEPER OF THE 'CLEAN HEART GRID'®

She works with Fortune 100 companies, governments, top executives and managers, cutting-edge health care researchers, pioneering educators, as well as world class athletes including Olympic Medalists and Olympic Coaches.

Ms. Woodsmall is also an expert in human typologies. She created the *International Research Institute for Human Typological Studies,* specializing in research on human difference. Here the emphasis is the connection between human differences and performance and the shaping of cultures to create high performance organizations and global cooperation. She and her partner/husband design and implement organizational and culture-shaping projects to strengthen the productivity of people and technology, integrating socio-technical values models to enhance productivity in a world where the interconnectedness of people and technology demand innovative approaches to deal with change.

Her trainings and consulting work take her around the globe where she conducts workshops in entrepreneurship, creativity, learning, leadership, values, culture-shaping, stress and time management, sales, teambuilding, coaching, *People Patterns™ and Personality Language™,* performance enhancement for children, developing self-awareness, *Learning How to Learn™,* a variety of Typlogies, parenting, dealing with change, etc., to name a few, as well a variety of personal development workshops.

In the late eighties, Marilyne and her husband created *Learning How to Learn Technology™,* focusing on how people learn. Her trainings and workshops are part of *The CLWF Institute for Global Leadership* and *The Children of Light and Wisdom Foundation, Inc.,* of which she is the Visionary Founder (www.theclwf.org). Its mission is to develop enlightened global leaders and entrepreneurs capable of critical and creative thinking, using innovative learning and educational models and new technologies from different fields.

ABOUT THE AUTHOR

She is the Author and Co-Author of business, educational & personal growth/metaphysical books and CDs, and behavioral assessment tools.

Ms. Woodsmall is a Certified Teacher of three forms of Reiki and two other healing modalities. She is also a Certified Master Trainer of NLP and Master Modeler. She learned Feng Shui in the late 1980's before it was known in the US and continues to teach it to this day.

If you would like to make an appointment for a coaching session with Marilyne Woodsmall (the *Mind Coach*®), or for information about consulting, modeling projects and speaking engagements and workshops by Ms. Woodsmall, please contact her at: wisdomlady888@verizon.net.

www.mindbraintechnologies.com

www.mindbraintechnologies.com/slideshow

www.thefutureoflearning.com

www.themichelthomasmethod.com

www.personalitylanguage.com

www.peoplepatternpower.com

www.thescienceofidiots.com

www.thecleanheartgridnetwork.com

www.TheStoryofJaren.com

www.newmindsforthefuture.com

www.thechildrenoflightandwisdomfoundation.org

THE STORY OF JAREN:
KEEPER OF THE 'CLEAN HEART GRID'®

Made in the USA
Charleston, SC
14 February 2011